HELP *for the* HURTING FAMILY

BUILDING STRONG FAMILIES IN A CHAOTIC WORLD

Larry E. Banta, M.D.

WESTBOW
PRESS®
A DIVISION OF THOMAS NELSON
& ZONDERVAN

WestBow Press books may be ordered through booksellers or by contacting:

WestBow Press
A Division of Thomas Nelson & Zondervan
1663 Liberty Drive
Bloomington, IN 47403
www.westbowpress.com
844-714-3454

ISBN: 978-1-6642-7711-3 (sc)
ISBN: 978-1-6642-7710-6 (hc)
ISBN: 978-1-6642-7712-0 (e)

Library of Congress Control Number: 2022916183

Print information available on the last page.

WestBow Press rev. date: 09/14/2022

To pastors and counselors who work diligently to help
families become healthy and Christ-centered

CONTENTS

Introduction

One of society's main issues is the disintegrating family structure. This is evident in crime rates, orphaned and abandoned children, gangs, child trafficking, and especially the suicide rates. This has infected the church as well, with increasing divorce rates and many children leaving the faith after they have grown and left the nest. This is an urgent problem all over the world and in all cultures.

The role of the family in society and in the church is paramount to create and maintain a culture in which we are able to sustain our faith, pass the faith along, and maintain a stable moral base in the community. Strong Christian families affect the culture around them, even the nonbelievers, in a way that improves society. Ministry to the family should be one of the main activities of the local church in order to effectively minister to the community. Likewise, ministry to the family by the leaders of the family needs to be a priority in life.

There are many aspects to helping the family. We want to build strong families, and we want children to grow up to be productive, mature Christian adults who can then also pass the faith along to their progeny. We also strongly desire to prevent children from having to grow up away from their biological family; we want to prevent orphans and abandoned children.

Society today is built on an insecure foundation of secularism. There is often no belief in a personal God, no concrete principles on which to structure one's life and morals. This has resulted in moral relativism; that is, we make the rules, and the rules constantly change according to the dominant powers in place. There is no clear sense of identity or family structure. This results in the chaos with which we are surrounded.

Families are hurting and confused. They often are unable to fulfill the purpose of a family, or they don't have much purpose at all. This leaves the children unable to secure a firm identity and self-concept. They often don't see the purpose of leaving home and being on their own, taking on the adult responsibilities of family and a job, or becoming the spiritual leader of the family.

We are left with a weakened and chaotic family system with no direction, one that is in need of healing. We need to come back to the basic principles: seeking God and fulfilling His purpose.

In part I, we will build on the strong foundation of the Word of God. This is followed by a look at what the family system is and the structure that makes it effective.

We will then investigate and consider the various roles in the family, as defined by scripture, and how to strengthen those roles. We also will look at the important task of child-rearing, with the idea of leading our children to Christ, discipling them to maturity, and launching them successfully as adults.

In part II, we will take on the family challenges that the church sometimes misses. Many hurting people are not helped by the church and often are rejected. Divorce is very common and needs to be addressed, as well as single parenting and stress from custody battles, which are all too common. The church must be ready to address these challenges.

Then, there are the really tough issues that families and individuals face. What is the church's role with regard to the severely mentally ill or the disabled or families dealing with a disabled child, spouse, or other family members? How do we help the caregivers who are stressed and cannot get relief or get to worship services?

This is a troubled world with many conflicts and temptations that can destroy individuals; as a result, there are stressful family relationships. We need to effectively deal with sin, addiction, and other serious problems that can affect the life of the family and the effective witness that we all want to have.

To effectively minister to families, we need to look at the whole picture with all of the difficulties and challenges so that we can work toward the goal of ministering to even the special needs in difficult situations.

As a psychiatrist, I was trained in family therapy. I learned how to deal with troubled and hurting children and hurting, dysfunctional families, and I dealt with severe, chronic mental illness, as well as many neurologic illnesses. I have seen the destruction that sin brings into our lives and the consequences of not building our lives and families on the strong foundation of the Word of God. I have provided training for church leaders in many cultures to encourage them in strengthening families and dealing with the hard issues.

The goal of this book is to encourage and help pastors and church leaders in many cultures to more effectively address many of the concerns in family life and to provide the best care for our precious families. We want to help and encourage them to be strong and healthy and to promote healing for the hurting families. Many books and manuals detail how to fix broken families and difficult children, and they can be very helpful. The goal of this book is to lay the foundation to prevent many problems that would otherwise occur, which is part I. In part II, we look at some of the hard issues that need to be addressed. Our families need to be built on the strong foundation of God's Word and to be purpose-driven to accomplish what God has in mind for us and to deal with the reality of a fallen world and all it brings.

This book can be used as a guide for teaching families, as ideas for sermon topics or group teaching, or as a resource for training pastors and church leaders so that they will be aware of the challenges we face. This book will provide the foundation and some resources to help the families in the church to grow strong.

Strong families will result in a strong church and can even have a positive effect on the community and the culture as they see how we live in peace and care for one another.

> Dear friends, let us love one another, for love comes from God. Everyone who loves has been born of God and knows God. Whoever does not love does not know God, because God is love. (1 John 4:7–8)

PART ONE

CONSTRUCTING A HEALTHY FAMILY

1

The Foundation

To start a building project in a proper way, we need a good foundation. Building on sand does not work so well. A few years ago, while I was living on a thirty-acre ranch, I wanted to put an equipment shed on the property. The soil was very sandy to a rather significant depth. The builder insisted that the building would be anchored fine with some pegs that went only two feet into the sandy soil. I argued that the place where we lived had the name Sand Hollow for a reason. He insisted it would be fine. Only a few years later, with a strong gust of wind, the entire forty-eight-by-fifty-six-foot shed uprooted and moved across the driveway, taking out an electric pole, the transformer for the entire area, and a couple of good-sized trees. The builder lost a good deal of money in cleaning it up and rebuilding it with a proper foundation and anchoring.

We also need a strong foundation to maintain ourselves, our family, and our church, the household of God:

> So, then you are no longer strangers and aliens, but you are fellow citizens with the saints and members of the household of God, built on the foundation of the apostles and prophets, Christ Jesus himself being the cornerstone, in whom the whole structure, being joined together, grows into a holy temple in the Lord. (Ephesians 2:19ff)

Without a firm foundation, the structure does not stand. Tragedies result when buildings or houses are built on unstable land or with foundations that are not strong and not designed to hold those types of structure. Entire large buildings have collapsed in the street, killing many. Having a firm foundation and good instructions for living makes life a good deal better.

> Everyone who comes to me and hears my words and does them, I will show you what he is like: he is like a man building a house, who dug deep and laid the foundation on the rock. And when a flood arose, the stream broke against that house and could not shake it, because it had been well built. But the one who hears and does not do them is like a man who built a house on the ground without a foundation. When the stream broke against it, immediately it fell, and the ruin of that house was great. (Luke 6:48ff)

The Faulty Foundation

The world today wants to design a paradise that leaves God out. The foundation has no real structure. Morality is built on the foundation that *I* can decide what is wrong or right if *I* feel it is wrong or right, and that can change from day to day, depending on how *I* might feel. My origin, on this foundation, is that I somehow was evolved; therefore, there is no God. I am the highest authority over me. My purpose is vague, but mostly life is such that I need to be having fun, becoming as rich as possible, and doing all I can for myself to have a good life. My destiny is to go back to the dirt where I came from, which leaves very little hope.

The faulty foundation is built on the fluctuating standards of the world. We can see the results:

> Godlessness in the Last Days
> But understand this, that in the last days there will come times of difficulty. For people will be lovers of self, lovers of money, proud, arrogant, abusive, disobedient to their

parents, ungrateful, unholy, heartless, unappeasable, slanderous, without self-control, brutal, not loving good, treacherous, reckless, swollen with conceit, lovers of pleasure rather than lovers of God, having the appearance of godliness, but denying its power. Avoid such people. For among them are those who creep into households and capture weak women, burdened with sins and led astray by various passions, always learning and never able to arrive at a knowledge of the truth. Just as Jannes and Jambres opposed Moses, so these men also oppose the truth, men corrupted in mind and disqualified regarding the faith. But they will not get very far, for their folly will be plain to all, as was that of those two men. (2 Timothy 3:1–9)

Let's look at the some of the components of this foundation (based on the Greek definitions from *Strong's Exhaustive Concordance*):

- "lovers of self": self-centered or selfish (2 Timothy 3:2); an undue sparing of self with the primary concern that things be easy and pleasant for oneself.
- "lovers of money": avaricious, covetous.
- "proud": a wandering about; a boaster.
- "arrogant": proud; often associated with the rejection of God.
- "abusive": the original meaning is blasphemous, sluggish, slow, or stupid; to be abusive is to revile or destroy one's good name.
- "disobedient to their parents": dishonoring, disrespecting, or not heeding their directives; unwilling to be persuaded.
- "ungrateful": without showing favor or kindness; unthankful.
- "unholy/ungodly": no regard of duty to God or humankind.
- "heartless": without family love.
- "unappeasable": does not abide by a truce; wants to keep on fighting.
- "slanderous": accusatory; a false accuser, used for the devil.
- "without self-control": incontinent; unable to govern one's appetites.
- "brutal": not mild; ungentle; fierce.

- "not loving good": not loving those who love good; not a lover of being good.
- "unfriendly": hostile; a person who may have pity but does not necessarily do anything to relieve the suffering of another through self-denial.
- "treacherous": deceitful; not able to be trusted.
- "reckless": impulsive; not stopping to think before initiating an action.

The scripture clearly tells us what are the fruits of the faulty foundation:

> The acts of the flesh are obvious: sexual immorality, impurity and debauchery; idolatry and witchcraft; hatred, discord, jealousy, fits of rage, selfish ambition, dissensions, factions and envy; drunkenness, orgies, and the like. (Galatians 5:19–21)

The faulty foundation produces fruit that does no one any good; it produces harm to the person, family, society, and culture. What is your foundation? Are you firmly rooted and grounded in His Word? Are you leaving yourself open to temptation and deception? But if your foundation is solid, it will flourish like the tree planted by the water:

> Blessed is the one
> who does not walk in step with the wicked
> or stand in the way that sinners take
> or sit in the company of mockers,
> but whose delight is in the law of the Lord,
> and who meditates on his law, day and night.
> That person is like a *tree planted by streams of water,*
> which yields its fruit in season
> and whose leaf does not wither—
> whatever they do prospers.
> Not so the wicked!
> They are like chaff
> that the wind blows away.

Therefore, the wicked will not stand in the judgment,
nor sinners in the assembly of the righteous.
For the LORD watches over the way of the righteous,
but the way of the wicked leads to destruction. (Psalm 1,
emphasis added)

On the solid foundation our fruit is something very positive:

But the fruit of the Spirit is love, joy, peace, forbearance,
kindness, goodness, faithfulness, gentleness and self-
control. Against such things there is no law. Those who
belong to Christ Jesus have crucified the flesh with its
passions and desires. Since we live by the Spirit, let us
keep in step with the Spirit. Let us not become conceited,
provoking and envying each other. (Galatians 5:22–26)

When presented with something we need to assemble or repair, we are
far better off to read the instructions so we can complete the job properly.
God has given us instructions in His Word that are for our good and for
the good of our world. The strong foundation of His Word gives us the
operating instructions for ourselves, our families, and our church. God has
a plan. In the Bible, He provided all the instructions we need to fulfill that
plan. The foundation for the church and for society is the *family* whose
foundation is Jesus.

God's plan is

- that we build and strengthen our families on the solid rock of
  Jesus,
- that we pass our faith along to our children, and
- that our children grow into productive, committed Christian
  adults who, in turn, will pass the faith to their offspring.

God's plan for us includes the following:

- Trust
- Obedience
- Faithful service

- Blessings
- Fruitful life
- Heaven

Satan's plan is to

- spread mistrust and convince us that the Bible is not true or not completely true;
- promote self-interest ("I am number one; I deserve; I need; I want");
- make sin acceptable ("Surely God will understand; it is not really that bad");
- promote violence;
- destroy the family by taking God out of the family, diluting the authority of the parents; promoting conflicts, arguments, and anger; and destroying values and morality (if the Bible is not true, then anything goes!);
- make use of you to promote the above and then destroy your own family and others; and then
- destroy you when he is done with you.

Satan's plan for us includes the following:

- Doubt
- Distraction
- Deception
- Deployment
- Destruction

In order to build a strong, resilient family, we need to look at all the parts that comprise a family system. In the next section, we will explore the concept of systems—how things work together for a particular function. As a functional healthy family system, we are like a machine with its many parts that work together to fulfill a particular purpose. Based on the understanding of the family system, we will see how the structure of a healthy family can be built in that system. The system and structure must be built on the foundation of the Word of God.

2

Systems and Structure: Building on the Foundation

With our foundation in Christ and the Word of God, we now are ready to start building the family. In order to fully understand how to create and manage a healthy and effective family, it is important to understand some basics about how things work in general.

Understanding the concept of systems will help you be a better, more productive part of the family system in which you live. Following the explanation of systems, you can then see how the family structure fits within the system to operate in a way that is efficient and functional.

If you look at a car or motorcycle, you can see that it works only as a result of its collection of parts—all assembled correctly, all doing their assigned tasks, and all working efficiently. If even one part is not working well, the machine might not run, at least not to its full effect. Each part is important and plays a role. If you neglect your car or motorcycle for a long time, it will eventually fall apart and no longer be useful. If you do not maintain its oil and other fluids, keep it clean, and regularly lubricate the moving parts, it will soon be of no use to you. If you leave a nicely built barn to the elements, soon it will start to decay and fall apart:

Whenever humans gather to achieve a common purpose or goal, they also are working as a system—a human system but very much like the mechanical system described above. The family is one of the systems in which we live and work. In a human system, there are the following elements. The following is adapted from the various works of Fritjof Capra on systems theory:

Components: These are the parts, all the individuals working in the same system.

Roles: This is similar to a job title.

Responsibilities: These are the particular things that each must do to keep things going. This is like a job description.

Relationships: This is about how we respond to one another, and it defines our connections, whether husband-wife, child-parent, child-teacher, or child-caregiver; in a job, boss-employee, supervisor-worker, administrator-personnel.

Hierarchy: Some roles have more responsibility than others; some are in charge of various aspects of the system to make it work well. Others have the duties assigned by those who are in charge. This extends to the parent-child relationship—parents, not the children, are in charge.

Boundaries: This defines the rules for the relationships, how one properly interacts with the other, and common courtesies and greetings, as well as levels of intimacy.

The family system is designed for a purpose. All the components of the system, when system is working in a healthy manner, will work together to fulfill the purpose of the system.

It requires energy to make a system work. Each person, doing his or her part, instills energy into the system, causing it to become better organized and more functional. Each one taking on his or her role keeps the system from dragging so it operates at optimum levels. Each one in the system who remains predominantly positive in attitude spreads an energy to the rest that is contagious in a good way. If we avoid conflict and are not critical, this promotes harmony in the system, and it functions like a well-oiled machine toward accomplishing our purpose.

In the study of physics, the science of how physical things work, there is a law called the second law of thermodynamics—a big name but a simple concept. What it basically says is that everything tends to become disorganized and tends toward chaos. If you do not put energy into something, it will proceed on a path to self-destruction. This is true for your car or motorcycle, as well as for your church, school, or work, or even your own body. It is likewise true for the family. If you care for and keep up maintenance on a nice house, it can last for many years:

As a part of the system, you must define your roles and responsibilities. This is often done with a job description in the working world, which helps to define what you do as your part. Learn your role well. Completing your role and fulfilling your tasks in a way that brings honor to God will keep the system working well. Encouraging others in their roles also adds energy to the system and causes it to work better. The following scripture concurs in this matter:

> Whatever you do, work at it with all your heart, as working
> for the Lord, not for human masters. (Colossians 3:23)

Doing it with heart and putting your whole self into the ministry of the family will produce the success that is needed. For the family system to work well and harmoniously, it needs to have a defined goal and purpose. The main goal of a Christian family is to produce productive, committed Christian adults. Anything you do while focusing on that goal will help to bring it about.

As an integral part of the system, you must constantly examine yourself to see if you are fulfilling your roles and responsibilities and supporting others in fulfilling theirs. In addition, if you can be a positive and encouraging influence on your family members, you will fulfill your part *and* add positive energy and organization to the family system. Search your heart before God to make sure you are contributing to the system's success.

Another important concept in understanding systems is that a system is either *endothermic* (consuming energy) or *exothermic* (producing energy). A healthy family system produces energy that all members enjoy. Dad and Mom come home and then are recharged to do what they need to do at work or to deal with household duties. Children come home from school and get charged up for the next day. Adult children come back and get recharged from the parents. The energy that is produced can allow the members of the family to give to others in reaching out and helping those who are struggling. So not only do you have the effective ministry to each other at home, but it goes beyond when the system is working well.

In the endothermic system, the components/members come home to stress and tension and go out each day with less energy than they came in with. They have no energy to reach out to others and no energy driving the system toward health, only strife and conflict. Members needing energy may seek it in the wrong places. This is not a productive system, and without help, it will not survive.

Understanding these basic concepts reminds us to focus on our parts and to do our best.

Now understanding that we work together as a system to fulfill God's purpose in this ministry, we need to see how to actually build and maintain the system and structure necessary. We will start with understanding how to structure the home so the system works. Maintaining structure requires positive energy input.

Keep in mind that everything tends toward chaos, and Satan wants to help it go that way!

God's plan is harmony and integrity. He will keep it going that way as long as you keep your focus on Him.

Structure

To design the proper foundation to run a home, we must have *structure*. This is like the framing of a house or its inner workings. It is within this framework that the home operates. Without this structure the home nothing more than a collection of people living in chaos.

The following is adapted from my book *Effective Orphan Care Ministry* (2015):

A structured home has the following qualities:

- Consistency
- Predictability
- Security
- Positive relationships
- Healthy growth and development

Let's take a look at these qualities:

Consistency means events and daily activities are generally by routine, on time, and expected—the day has some sort of regular pattern. Things occur, most of the time, in a manner of *predictability*. There is a sense of *security*, as the patterns allow the children and adults to be comfortable and know what to expect. Things are organized and arranged in a secure way, and this, in turn, allows *positive relationships* to develop. From this foundation, the family members feel safe and experience *healthy growth and development*.

If we recall the basics of systems theory, found at the beginning of this chapter, we can see that the family is a system. A system works to fulfill a purpose. As such, left on its own without conscious care, it will tend to disorganize and fall apart, much the same as an old car left out in the weather or an old neglected barn no longer used. To make the system work, energy is needed. This reverses the tendency toward chaos and serves to develop and maintain *integrity*. Integrity is oneness, wholeness—all parts of the system operating together and well, allowing the machine to function properly to fulfill its purpose.

By maintaining structure, we then maintain system integrity. Structure creates the environment in which the system can function. Since all systems have a purpose, the family system can then generate its product—committed, productive Christian adults. When the system is not functioning, the product is destructive, rather than constructive. Our role is to do our part to keep the system running smoothly.

What does proper structure do?

- Children raised in an organized family system learn to properly manage themselves in the world.
- They gain moral grounding, learn to be patient and tolerate delayed gratification, and are less likely to be impulsive and hyperactive.
- They acquire drive and motivation.
- They are more likely to have healthy biological rhythms.
- They are likely to be better in control of their emotions.
- They are more likely to have a clear understanding and respect for proper boundaries.

Children who come from chaotic or abusive backgrounds often lack proper tracts in the brain for modulating biorhythms and emotional control. When we think of what chaos and inattention produce, we can imagine that one growing up with that would learn to be chaotic and without his or her own internal structure. This produces a poor moral foundation. "I want what I want right now!" The result is also someone who cannot control impulses and may be more hyperactive.

As family structure falls apart, we see a great increase in children with behavior problems. These children also lack future orientation—that is, they do not dream of the future, plan ahead, or think about the consequences of their decisions. Emotions tend to be either flat and unexpressive or without proper context and boundaries. The children are more likely to exhibit symptoms often thought to be from major mental illness (sometimes this is the case, but not always).

The sense of boundaries is taught within the context of structure. Without such, it is hard to know what the rules are. Looking at the systems that seem to be affected by lack of structure, could it be that structure affects brain development? That is, indeed, the case. External structure produces internal structure—this is an important concept to remember.

External structure produces internal structure.

- External structure will gradually become internalized as the child lives within and responds to the system.
- The process of internalizing structure allows for the development of the proper brain tracts.
- All learning produces new connections or tracts in the brain.

Learning new things changes the structure of the brain by promoting the development of new tracts, like wires, between various areas of the brain so the person is thus able to act differently. Without structure, children do not have the proper tracts and connections in the brain to modulate emotions and behaviors or even their biological rhythms—when to eat, sleep, go to the bathroom, and so forth.

As the child lives within the structure, the external gradually becomes internal. The structure promotes tracts, new learning, and a change in how the child operates. The longer the structure remains in place and the more consistent it is, the more consistently tracts or brain connections develop.

Understanding what structure is and how we can create it and maintain it is a very important part of healthy parenting. The concept of the home as a system helps us understand how we can create the needed structure. The structure of the home includes the following key elements:

- Discipline
- Scheduling
- Rituals
- Boundaries
- Hierarchy
- Roles and responsibilities

Now we'll take a closer look at each of these key elements.

Discipline

- Teach what is good and proper at every chance you get.
- Apply consequences to behavior that are consistent, appropriate to the situation, just, nonabusive, and understandable to the child.
- Keep discipline positive as much as possible.
- Point out what is incorrect or inappropriate; this provides opportunities to quickly turn the focus on correct, appropriate behaviors.
- Look for teachable moments.
- Catch children being good; this helps to provide positive affirmation.

Before we can teach what is proper, we must have a foundation of morality that comes from the Word of God. If we lack understanding of His Word, we ourselves do not have the fundamentals to pass on to the children. There would be no basis on which to make any moral decisions. Morality would be based on our own human ideas, which are highly subject to change.

It takes energy to be vigilant, to notice when things are not right and make adjustments, to provide guidance, and to consistently manage consequences through to completion. As we apply consequences, we must always think about what we are doing:

What is the goal of the consequence? To teach? To cause pain and affliction? To get revenge for something the child did against me?

Always, the goal must be to teach and train. This is why sometimes we need to back off and consider before taking action. Maybe we could ask the advice of others, or better yet, turn to God in a peaceful prayer for guidance so our reaction does not promote negativity and make things worse. Consequences must be consistently applied, must be appropriate to the situation, and must have the goal of training the child.

To understand the purpose of discipline, we need to understand the concept of *discipling*—that is, helping our children become followers of Jesus. Always keep in mind the goal of producing productive adult Christians. Are the consequences you apply likely to draw children closer to God or to push them away from Him? Look forward to moments of discipline as *teachable moments*, when a positive influence can have a potent effect.

Also look for teachable moments when quick lessons can be powerfully provided, especially during times of good behavior. Catching kids in their good moments takes a bit of conscious effort, but it is worthwhile. Providing a few quick words of encouragement is powerful in promoting good behavior. They'll appreciate that you noticed and will remember that feeling for a long time!

Scheduling

Some families do well with maintaining a regular schedule. In our fast-paced world, however, it is easy to just let things slide. It is important to recognize *why* we need scheduling. It is not just for convenience, although it does help the system run smoothly. It affects the process of attachment and normal development. Providing a consistent pattern in the day, when the child has expectations of certain things happening predictably, reduces anxiety and allows the development of trust, a major component necessary for healthy attachment, which is a necessary part of development for the child.

Proper scheduling requires energy and dedication. Once again, energy applied to the situation organizes the system and reduces chaos. Chaos sucks up energy, producing more chaos, and eventually results in a breakdown of the system.

Consistent bedtimes, mealtimes, and awakening times assist in keeping the system running smoothly. We understand that there are always exceptions to the rules for special occasions and circumstances. We would thereafter return to the normal scheduling.

Following a schedule changes the way the brain works; it improves growth, mood stability, and sleep patterns.

A note on family mealtime: in many cultures, including in the USA, the concept of dining together is gradually disappearing, as each member of the family is busy with his or her activities. Mealtime is essential for maintaining communication, discussing important topics, and having a good time together; it is a time to be thankful for all of God's provision. The meal must be attended without the common electronic devices that so many have.

Rituals

Rituals produce a sense of community and belonging. Portions of cultural and personal identities are tied to rituals. It is important to put energy into regularly observing events so as to develop and maintain important parts of the identity. It also provides an opportunity to do important and meaningful activities together as a family.

Be creative to make it interesting. Make sure you understand what the ritual means and how important it is to perpetuate.

Cultural rituals help maintain a sense of identity. These practices celebrate belonging to a particular culture and provide an important sense of identity and history. Some cultural rituals include what we do as Christians—the main identity we wish to instill in our children.

Daily rituals include prayer before meals. As we sit down to a meal, rather than chaotically diving into the provided food, attention is requested. Everyone assumes a prayer stance, whether holding hands, folding hands, or bowing the head to show reverence to God. All are quiet, while one addresses our Lord in a respectful manner. This reminds us all that every good gift comes from God—all our provisions, food, money, shelter, everything is from Him, and to Him we owe gratitude.

Mealtime prayer and devotion assist with putting God in His rightful place in our minds and hearts: on His throne, in charge of the universe, as the one who keeps us and provides for us. That is part of the hierarchy that is very much needed in the Christian home.

Devotion time should be before bed or in the morning. As we end the day, we may gather for prayer, or we may start the day with Bible reading and prayer. Devotion time needs to have some flexibility so that spiritual questions can be addressed briefly, together as a family, and maybe to offer time individually to those who struggle in any area.

How do we greet one another throughout the day? Proper greetings help maintain the adult-child hierarchy. In American culture, we do not hold so much to the greeting as in nearly every other culture, but it remains important in America as well. Prior to addressing adults, children need to learn to extend a respectful "good morning," "good afternoon," or "good evening." In Asian cultures, there might be a bow; in other cultures, a handshake. Children learn what is appropriate to their culture, and this helps establish proper boundaries and respect. Part of the ritual is also to learn to not interrupt unless it is an urgent matter. Maintaining rituals emphasizes the hierarchy and promotes proper boundaries and respect for one another.

Special Rituals

Special rituals occur only occasionally, usually once per year. We must put energy into making these days special, as they can bring the family together to provide that sense of belonging and that each one is important; that our nation and culture are important.

- Birthdays: This is a special time for each member of the family. Even if the family lacks economic resources for an elaborate celebration, something special can be done—maybe a cake or special dessert, a song, or a time to share together. As a part of this ritual, a prayer can be offered for the special one but one in which a special blessing on his or her life is offered, with special concern for the upcoming year and that he or she will remain close to Jesus.

- Anniversaries: Recognize special days with special meanings, such as the parents' wedding anniversary or other special anniversaries. This is a good excuse for a bit of cake or other treat and a special prayer of blessing.

- Christmas: Most of the world's Christians celebrate the birth of our Savior in some way. The type of celebration might vary substantially from place to place, but it is a special day. How one celebrates mostly depends on the culture in one's location and perhaps according to some family rituals. There might be gift giving or special treats for everyone. The main event, however, needs to be the reading of the Christmas story in Luke 2:1–20 and lively discussion about the amazing thing God did by sending His Son to save us. Developing a ritual for the occasion is meaningful and impactful to children. Avoiding the pagan side of the celebration is important, as well as not making it too materialistic.

- Resurrection Sunday: Though many of us celebrate the Resurrection each Sunday and memorialize it with the Lord's Supper, many areas celebrate a special day during the year to recognize the Resurrection of Jesus. There might be cultural differences, but it is important to incorporate the story of the Resurrection with time to reflect on it, to remember the great sacrifice that was made on our behalf, and the overcoming of death with the victory of His Resurrection. It is a joyous occasion and needs to be celebrated as such. It is essential that we avoid the associated pagan rituals for what was, in many cultures, a converted pagan holiday.

- National holidays: God has made it clear that we should "honor the king." First Peter 2:17 states, "Show proper respect to everyone, love the family of believers, fear God, honor the emperor." This means that we must respect our country and its leaders, obey the laws, and share in the special celebrations. This provides us a sense of belonging to our country and culture. Enjoy the day with culturally appropriate activities, along with some history lesson by way of a story that defines the reason for the celebration. As always, enjoy a wonderful opportunity to worship God, the almighty and true King.

- Special cultural days: Some cultures have other special days of observation. We need to be careful what these celebrate. Some are pagan and involve a type of reverence to false gods. We need to teach children about these but not involve ourselves in the celebrations. The parents must be familiar with the culture and what the various celebrations mean. This can be a time of teaching about the history of the culture and can be developed into a positive experience.

Rite of Passage Rituals

It is especially important to mark special rite of passage events that signal going from one stage of life to another. Each major step in life needs to be marked so that the idea is etched in our minds that we have shifted from one set of circumstances to the next. "I was _____; now I am_____." With a new stage, new responsibilities are present, and rites of passage signify readiness to face those responsibilities.

- *Graduation from kindergarten, primary school, high school, or college.* Marking the accomplishment not only serves to improve self-esteem and self-image, but it also readies the child for the next important stage. She or he passes to a new stage of life with new challenges.
- *Preteen and teen birthdays, a special time to discuss sexuality and development.* This might be around the twelfth or thirteenth birthday. Some families provide a special time for those reaching this stage, at which time they can be instructed in sexuality— what is right and wrong and how to resist the temptation to adopt others' lack of morality. This can be combined with athletic events, special outings, or other special activities. (See chapter 9, "Sexuality Education in the Home.")
- *Blessings—special prayers and affirmations at special times.* When the family member celebrates something special, it is very important to ask God's blessing on his or her life and future direction. This helps us to see how important God is in our lives and futures

and that we should to continue to lean on Him for the help and guidance we need. (Consider reading *The Blessing: Giving the Gift of Unconditional Love and Acceptance* by John Trent and Gary Smalley.)

- *Photographs.* Another way to assist in the sense of belonging in the family is the use of photographs and albums to memorialize events, celebrations, and stages in life. Pictures can be displayed in the home and changed as new things happen. Scrapbooking is also a way to recall the important events in the life of the family. Having a scrapbook or photo album that the child can take with him or her when he or she launches into independent living is a special way to stay connected as a family.

Boundaries

Boundaries are defined by the particular rules in the family and culture. These help us to relate in a way that is comfortable and appropriate and that values the position of each one in the family.

- Interpersonal space: This is often culturally defined but generally is gauged according to our own comfort levels. We need to maintain proper space and only enter someone's personal space when given permission to do so. Interpersonal space is like an invisible bubble around us. Someone else can be close but not too close.
- Greetings: This helps us to maintain proper social distance. Greetings, as mentioned previously, also help keep the hierarchy in place.
- Respect for property: We must maintain respect for our own property and also have respect for others' property. Searching an older child's room should be done only when there is a specific reason, such as suspected drugs or contraband or thoughts of self-harm or causing harm to others. There might be situations in which increased vigilance is necessary to keep the child or others from harm.
- Touching: A touch to the arm or shoulder can be comforting and appreciated. Inappropriate touching that could be considered sexual can greatly disturb the child.

- Language: Verbal language must be proper and not wander into vulgarities or inappropriate areas, such as sexuality, unless specific questions are asked, which then are best addressed by a same-sex parent, if available. Inappropriate language must be noted and corrected; generally, verbal correction is adequate. Many children will pick up the bad language from their peers and must be instructed as to what is proper and what is not.
- Appropriate sexuality: Maintaining appropriate boundaries between parents and children, as well as between the children, is vitally important. Children may learn their behavior from peers and will need to be corrected and shown the proper way. Appropriate touching and teaching about privacy and respecting one's own body must be a part of the general teaching in the home.
- Privacy: This relates to the child's personal space, as well as an understanding of modesty and personal possessions. Parents should not invade a child's privacy unless warranted, as noted above.
- Hierarchy: This is the defined level of authority in the family system. Parents have defined roles and are at a higher level. The the children also have a role under the protection and guidance of the parents. Everything works much better when each is able to be in his or her proper role.

It is important for the parents to maintain the position of being in charge; children are not. All battles must be won by parents so choose the battles wisely—remember, love *always* wins. When there is a power vacuum—that is, the parents are not in charge; are passively parenting; are not putting energy into their roles—the children then take control. This results in chaos and confusion.

When there are clear lines of authority, the system is much more secure. Each individual needs to know his or her role—the children are children; adults are in charge. When we must engage in battles, it is important to make sure that they are fair and that the outcome does not place the child in charge. It does not change the hierarchy for us to admit an honest mistake and seek the child's forgiveness; it serves to strengthen the relationship and maintain the hierarchy. There also needs to be room for discussing the reasons for decisions that we make. To maintain the hierarchy, the parents must continually be strong and effective as leaders. Jesus taught us the concept of servant leadership; this is how leadership works in the family as well.

Finally, in order to keep the family system healthy, each one must have defined roles and responsibilities:

- The role of the child is to play, learn, grow, and interact appropriately with others. As children are able, more work-related tasks should be assigned to teach more responsibility.
- The role of the parent is to be in charge and to manage the home with care and love, keeping the structure intact and functional, which requires a good bit of invested energy.

Important Concepts

- The family is a system.
- All systems tend toward chaos.
- Energy is required to maintain system integrity or wholeness.
- System integrity begins with the structure.
- Structure is what we do to allow the system to fulfill its purpose.
- The purpose of the Christian family system is to produce healthy, committed, productive Christian adults who will continue the process.

Conclusion

Understanding the concept of systems—how things work, the structure, the framework, the nuts and bolts of a functional family—can help us to keep our families strong and healthy.

Providing positive energy to the system involves fulfilling our roles, communicating well with other members, confirming boundaries, providing positive affirmation (energy) to other family members, and doing our part to maintain structural integrity.

Positive energy invested in the system produces system integrity (wholeness), which then allows the structure to persist so that its purpose is maintained.

Negative energy destroys the system's integrity, produces chaos, and alters the system's purpose, making the system run poorly; it does not produce the results desired.

The purpose of the family system is to produce productive, committed Christian adults.

Ideally, the family system would consist of both parents, but many times, due to divorce or death, one parent is left to do the job of both; this is difficult but can be done. It is still important to maintain the structure as much as possible to have the best outcome.

The concept of a healthy system and having a structured home also will assist in maintaining a healthy marriage, reducing stress and anxiety, and making the entire system stronger so it can withstand the challenges of life in a broken sinful world.

A healthy, productive family system not only looks after its own needs but can help with the needs of others in the church, community, or even other parts of the world.

3

The Role of the Man

A healthy family is one in which all members fulfill their roles. Men have a special role and are very much needed to fulfill that role so that the family can be successful. In many cultures, some inner-city areas, and some impoverished areas, fathers do not have much of a role. When I've spoken to people who work in the prison system, they have said that many of the inmates did not have a father figure in their lives. In my own experience as a psychiatrist and psychotherapist, those clients without a strong father figure have been at risk for problems in their lives.

What if the man does not fulfill his role? Consider the following:

- The family will lack a strong anchor and sense of security.
- Children may grow up insecure.
- Girls may seek to fill that father role in their lives in all the wrong places.
- Some may try to fill the void caused by lack of a father by joining gangs or looking for criminal or drug-related activities.
- Children may have a lack of a moral framework (not feeling the need to follow the rules of society).
- It can be difficult for children to understand the concept of Father God.
- When children become adults, they may be less likely to maintain stable employment.

- Society and culture deteriorate, as boys do not grow up into positive, responsible male role models.

According to scriptures, men need to do the following:

1. Leave and cleave! Leave their parents and cling to their wives. This basically means that as a young adult, a man leaves the parental home and connects and attaches to the wife and lives with her.

   Therefore, a man shall leave his father and his mother and hold fast to his wife, and they shall become one flesh. (Genesis 2:24)

   Therefore a man shall leave his father and mother and hold fast to his wife, and the two shall become one flesh. (Ephesians 5:31)

2. The husband must love his wife.

   Husbands, love your wives, just as Christ loved the church and gave himself up for her to make her holy, cleansing her by the washing with water through the word, and to present her to himself as a radiant church, without stain or wrinkle or any other blemish, but holy and blameless. In this same way, husbands ought to love their wives as their own bodies. He who loves his wife loves himself. After all, no one ever hated their own body, but they feed and care for their body, just as Christ does the church—for we are members of his body. "For this reason, a man will leave his father and mother and be united to his wife, and the two will become one flesh." This is a profound mystery—but I am talking about Christ and the church. However, each one of you also must love his wife as he loves himself, and the wife must respect her husband. (Ephesians 5:25–33)

   Husbands, love your wives, and do not be harsh with them. (Colossians 3:19)

Loving is an active process. God did not just sit up in heaven and feel all kinds of loving feelings about the sinners down here on earth. He loved actively by sending Jesus and continues to be active in our lives after we come to faith in Him. He is always working with and for us. The husband must love as Christ loved. That is a tall order, but the main issue is that he seeks the best for his wife. He is actively involved in expressing that type of unselfish, sacrificial love.

3. The husband must enjoy life with his wife.

> Enjoy life with the wife whom you love, all the days of your vain life that he has given you under the sun, because that is your portion in life and in your toil at which you toil under the sun. (Ecclesiastes 9:9)

How do we accomplish this? The wife needs to be the husband's best friend

- Work (toil) at keeping the relationship strong.
- Keep open communication so that there is enjoyment in conversation.
- Spend enjoyable time together, talking, walking, attending entertainment.

4. The husband must provide physical fulfillment with his wife.

> The husband should fulfill his marital duty to his wife, and likewise the wife to her husband. The wife does not have authority over her own body but yields it to her husband. In the same way, the husband does not have authority over his own body but yields it to his wife. Do not deprive each other except perhaps by mutual consent and for a time, so that you may devote yourselves to prayer. Then come together again so that Satan will not tempt you because of your lack of self-control. (1 Corinthians 7:3–5)

What are the marital duties? Intimacy is the main one. Intimacy is much more than the physical relationship; it is *closeness*, something deeper than friendship. We are *commanded* to keep the intimacy alive!

In order to have intimacy, we need to feed the relationship, treating each other with respect, opening up about heartaches and difficulties, and sharing moments of laughter and enjoyment. When we have this closeness, we can enjoy the sexual relationship. We are to make it enjoyable for both. The man seeks what is enjoyable for her, the woman does the same for her husband. Communicating likes and dislikes are very important, especially as you begin the journey together.

There should be regular intimacy, unless physical problems or spiritual problems prevent it.

It must *never* be forced.

5. The husband must live with the wife with understanding.

Learn how a woman thinks and functions. This means that we men need to make a study of how to understand women. We ask questions. We might even find some reading material that is helpful, such as James Dobson's *What Wives Wish Their Husbands Knew about Women* or Dr. John Gray's *Men Are from Mars, Women Are from Venus.* (See bibliography.)

> Likewise, husbands, live with your wives in an understanding way, showing honor to the woman as the weaker vessel, since they are heirs with you of the grace of life, so that your prayers may not be hindered. (1 Peter 3:7)

I grew up without sisters, so I found that the process of learning how a woman thinks and functions was a challenge. When I was dating my now-wife, I had to ask quite a few questions and get clarifications. During the first few years, I did some reading, and I talked with other men about how to keep the relationship strong and how to understand how she worked. Such an exploration can be quite interesting and enjoyable, if one is humble and open to learning new things.

6. He must provide for his own.

> But if anyone does not provide for his relatives, and
> especially for members of his household, he has denied
> the faith and is worse than an unbeliever. (1 Timothy 5:8)

The Bible is clear that if a man is able to work, he must. He is to provide for his own. He is to make an honest living. This involves the following:

- Finding and keeping a job
- Keeping the finances in order
- Keeping the priorities of finances in order
- Providing an offering to God
- Taking care of essential needs
- Saving for emergencies, if he can
- Budgeting for family time together; enjoying a vacation or a special meal or just being together in meaningful activity.
- Having an open discussion with his wife about money

7. The husband must provide leadership and protection for the family.

Scripture tells us that the man serves under the leadership of Jesus to then be the leader of the family.

> But I want you to understand that the head of every man
> is Christ, the head of a wife is her husband, and the head
> of Christ is God. (1 Corinthians 11:3)

He is to provide leadership, structure, and responsibility.

- Advise and counsel but always regard the input from the wife when considering decisions.
- Leadership is not control.
- Be a servant-leader, as Jesus demonstrated.

Providing protection for the family is also very important. First and foremost, pray for your family, but also be alert for harmful influences, and guide the family in the proper direction with regard to movies, books, entertainment, relationships, and negative spiritual influences.

Seek to understand what it means to be a servant-leader, and be ready to help with the duties around the house, offering a hand whenever needed or when you see a need you can fulfill. Be humble, listen to the wife and the children, and recognize your errors and seek forgiveness. Be a leader, demonstrating Christ's love to the family and to those outside the family.

8. He must fulfill the role.

The man, functioning under the authority and example of Christ and fulfilling his role in the family and in the church, can be a powerful influence in changing the culture, society, and the world and in adding energy to the family system. Energy is added by exerting a positive influence, fulfilling the role, encouraging others, and maintaining the structure of the family.

Passivity in the role of the father and husband has left many families without leadership and structure. Many have taken the role of provider as the main role or only role, leaving the other duties to the wife and maybe the older children. Others may not take even that responsibility.

Passivity means sitting on the sidelines, not directing, not providing words of encouragement, not teaching skills of living, not correcting misbehavior, not taking the children on special outings to do things together. This leaves a vacuum, and a vacuum seeks to be filled. Too often, the children and wife may seek other outlets to fill what is missing. This is a potent destroyer of families and an important cause of children not being well grounded or ready for life.

If a man is passive, he does not inject energy into the system, so the system will tend toward chaos and self-destruction.

In many cultures, we see situations where the father is relegated to having little purpose in the family. The role is taken over by the mother, as the father is not present—but he is not present because he does not have a role. It is vital that the role be created and sustained in the family system. When relegated to not having a role, the father will not stay connected to the family and will seek other ways to fulfill that vacuum.

4

The Role of the Woman

Throughout the Bible, God honors women in many ways. Women were the first to discover that Jesus was raised from the dead. Women were involved with the disciples in bringing the good news to many parts of the known world of that day. Throughout the centuries, strong, committed women were responsible for the growth of the church.

In many cultures, women are the first to respond to the gospel and later bring their families to faith in Christ. Women have a very important role in the church today, whether married or not. In the modern world, women have had changes in roles. In the past, many more women were homemakers, choosing not to work outside the home until the children were raised. Nowadays, in many cultures, women choose to work and also might have the responsibility of raising children. Many have to work. Many are single parents due to divorce or death of the husband. Later in this book, we will address some of the issues with single parenting.

Women may have many roles in the community and in the workforce, but here, I want to deal with the woman's role in the intact family. She has a key role in keeping the structure of the home intact, as well as parenting duties.

Proverbs 24:3–4 tells us:

> By *wisdom* a house is built,
> and through *understanding* it is established;

through *knowledge* its rooms are filled
with rare and beautiful treasures. (italics added)

We design and build a family with the foundation of the Word of God and with the system and structure as noted in the first part of this book.

The woman has a very important role in the structure of the home and the maintenance of that structure. She can provide the following:

- Wisdom: the capacity to see life the way God sees it
- Understanding: responding with good judgment
- Knowledge: learning with perception and insight, discovering, growing

So how does she acquire such capacities? It is a gradual process of lifelong growing and experiencing life in Christ. However, if one has the blessing of being raised in a Christian home, these lessons are generally taught. We learn so much from our parents, good and bad. In order to pass along a good foundation, there needs to be good female role models, a church home that teaches foundational truths of the Bible, and a community of Christians demonstrating those truths in their lives. As adults, we can also learn and acquire these skills. If we do not learn the basics as children, the church needs to provide help—the older women should teach the younger.

What are the consequences in a culture and society when women do not fulfill their roles?

- It is difficult for men to fulfill their roles.
- There is a lack of compassion.
- There can be a lack of common courtesy and politeness.
- There can be a definite lack of structure in the family.

In a two-parent family, the woman does much more for the maintenance of the structure, with such things as maintaining a schedule, routines, rituals, comfort, and a measure of security. Without maternal influence, the children often end up more anxious and insecure.

The woman must be supported in her roles by the man.

The man has a key role in the family. When he fulfills his family duties and takes his role seriously, it is easier for the woman to fulfill her important role.

Many scriptures help us to understand the role of the woman; the following scripture seems to summarize much of what is important in that role:

> Likewise, teach the older women to be reverent in the way they live, not to be slanderers or addicted to much wine, but to teach what is good. Then they can urge the younger women to love their husbands and children, to be self-controlled and pure, to be busy at home, to be kind, and to be subject to their husbands, so that no one will malign the word of God. (Titus 2:3–5)

Titus 2:3–5 helps us to see several of the important aspects of being a godly woman:

1. To be reverent in the way you live
    Show proper respect for the things of God—the church, the sacraments, the church leaders. Use proper, respectful language in all situations.

2. Not to be slanderers
    Have proper control of the tongue; do not speak ill of others.

3. Not to be addicted to substances, such as wine, or anything else that can become addictive—drugs, internet games, gambling, pornography, sex
    Anything that starts out as a sin can become an addiction—a continuing sin that will draw you away from God and from your family.

4. To teach what is good
    Be an example in word and deed to what is good and proper. Find moments in the family conversation to teach and train the children. Be an upright example for the husband, whether he is a believer or not.

5. To love your husband and children
   This is not optional, and it sometimes must be learned and promoted. At times, it is difficult. This is active love, in which you look for ways to please others without looking for a reward.

6. To be self-controlled and pure
   This is an example for the children and even the husband. Children always know what is going on. There are no secrets from children or from God. This attitude includes respect and courtesy in your interactions with others. It is infidelity if you cross boundaries in relationships with men other than your husband, even just flirting. You must maintain firm boundaries.

7. To be busy at home
   This means putting energy into the system, being a good manager of the home, and working hard to maintain the schedule and structure. Be a good administrator of money and resources. In the process of instilling energy into the family system and structure, it is also helpful to be creative in enlivening family life, cooking different meals, encouraging new activities, and so forth.

8. To be kind
   By exhibiting the fruit of the Spirit, you become a good representative of Christ in your life at home and in the community.

9. To be subject to your own husband
   Remember that the husband is required to love his wife as Christ loved the church, and so the woman subjects herself to a representative of Jesus. The husband has quite a responsibility before God to treat his wife very well. This subjection is only to your own husband and to the elders of the church with respect to the activities of the church and spiritual life, not just to anybody.

10. To grow in wisdom
    As the woman grows in wisdom and years, she can be one of the teachers and role models of the younger women.

It is important to recognize that the role is never intended to be something in which womanhood or the woman is disrespected.

- This does *not* imply being trampled; that is, being put down or controlled.
- This does *not* mean you lose your identity. You are an equal child of God.
- This does *not* imply domination by your husband. Servant leadership is humble leadership.
- This *does* mean treating others with respect, as though they are more important than yourself, and considering the needs of others as being important.
- This *does* mean supporting and respecting the decisions of your husband.
- This *does* mean providing your input into the decisions of the family but deferring to your husband for the final decision.
- This *does* mean being a good example to the honor and glory of our Lord.

If men take seriously the role of servant leader and the instruction to love their wives as Christ loved the church and gave Himself for it, there naturally would be a mutual respect. As problems arise, as they always will, there would be open discussion as to how to deal with the special circumstance. If the woman feels dominated or overcontrolled by her husband or has a sense that she is losing her identity, this may be a sign of current or impending domestic abuse. As a woman, you are not to get trampled; in the biblical role, you are respected. The woman maintains her precious identity in Christ. In supporting and respecting the husband, there should be no sense of being dominated.

> But for Adam no *suitable helper* was found. So, the LORD God caused the man to fall into a deep sleep; and while he was sleeping, he took one of the man's ribs and then closed up the place with flesh. Then the LORD God made a woman from the rib he had taken out of the man, and he brought her to the man. (Genesis 2:20–21, italics added)

The suitable helper is the person who is apt and sufficient to be the helper and companion of the husband.

It is important for the wife to strive to be exactly what the husband needs, helping him, supporting him, encouraging him, empathizing with his frustrations and disappointments, and rejoicing with him in his successes, as he rejoices with his wife and empathizes with her.

The Ministry of the Family, Calling and Mission

Each of us must take seriously the primary ministry that we have and to which we were called. That is to minister to our families first. This means the man is the leader and servant, and the woman is coleader and servant, under the authority of the man; the man is under the authority of Christ, and in that way, we minister to the children and to each other.

Are we ministering in the way God intends us to do?

Are there changes we need to make to have a more effective ministry in the family?

Change is hard but worthwhile. It involves our humbly calling on God to put energy into our systems through us and then that we do our parts to make and maintain the changes.

In the previous chapter, the concept of being a passive parent was discussed. This is equally true in the role of the woman. A passive woman— one who chooses to relinquish her duties as wife and mother and goes about with her friends, leaving the care of the family to others—will also deeply affect the function and purpose of the family. Often, children are raised by secular schools and daycare, in which values contrary to the Word of God are taught, and these are not addressed at home. If mothers and fathers take an active and necessary role in the education of the children, these influences can be countered effectively.

One effective countermeasure is a group called Moms in Prayer International (https://momsinprayer.org), in which mothers gather to pray and intercede for their children in the secular schools. (See bibliography at the end of this book.)

5

Preparing for Marriage

Most of our Western churches have guidelines for preparing for marriage and will offer counseling to help a couple get started in a good way. Most of the time with a proper foundation and a good dating experience, the couple can see if they are a good fit.

In the current post-Christian Western culture, it is becoming the norm for a couple to date a time or two, have a sexual relationship, move in together, and then, after some months or years, decide to get married. This has infiltrated the church, as children are taught this throughout their early lives. They see neighbors who are not married, or others in their class live with a parent who may have successive boyfriends or girlfriends pop in and out of their lives. This is very unstable and does not serve to create or maintain the strong foundation in the Word. God has expectations, and if we are believers, having accepted Christ, and call Him Lord, we need to follow His directions.

There is a local culture that leads us in a direction that often is not good, and there is a Christian culture that we must follow, wherever we might live. There may be differences in cultures with regard to dating, arranged marriages, and other situations, but the main thing is that we follow the scriptures with regard to how to live prior to and during marriage.

To help create a strong foundation as a couple, the church needs to provide a number of tasks as the spiritual connection in the lives of the couple who looks to marry. Premarital counseling is outlined in a number of fine books, which need to be used as a reference. As a guideline, what are the factors that we must cover?

1. There should be a strong foundation in the Word of God. If the couple lacks this, they need to make efforts to get on track spiritually. (See chapter 1 and the bibliography at the end of this book.)

2. Basic guidelines for dating should already be in place from youth group and parental teaching. (See chapter 9, "Sexuality Education in the Home.") The couple needs to set appropriate boundaries to stay safe from getting physically involved.

3. The couple must start with verbal communication. They should involve themselves in activities that allow for appropriate and sometimes deep conversation. They should ask each other questions to learn as much as possible about each other, including expectations of the eventual marriage. A particularly good book on this topic is *101 Questions to Ask before You Get Engaged* by H. Norman Wright. (See the bibliography.) It is a good book to have on hand.

4. There are many guides for the pastor in providing premarital counseling. One that I recommend is *Before You Say I Do* by H. Norman Wright. Assisting the couple in going through the steps in this book will help set them on the right footing.

Issues that the pastor or counselor needs to cover in preparing for marriage are as follows:

- Spiritual beliefs
- How to have a meaningful discussion; problem solving
- The couples' likes and dislikes
- What gets each one angry
- How to manage money
- Dealing with stress and difficulties
- Prayer and devotional life
- Mutual respect
- Forgiveness; how to let go of past hurts

- Any health issues that might affect life in the future
- Learning about each other's extended family

The above points help to solidify the foundation as the couple gets started on their journey. Too often, the foundation is laid with a physical attraction, premature intimacy, and with someone the individual doesn't really know. The marriage will be off to a rocky start, as the couple only then finds out who they really married.

Cognitive Errors

Some items that the church needs to clear up that are taught by the world are as follows:

- I must live with my partner to see if we are compatible before we get married.
- We must like the same things.
- We must never argue.
- Sex is the most important part of the marriage.
- I must win every argument.
- Divorce is always an option if we cannot work things out.

God clearly tells us that sex outside the marriage is wrong, a sin against Him and our own bodies.

> Flee from sexual immorality. All other sins a man commits
> are outside his body, but he who sins sexually sins against
> his own body. (1 Corinthians 6:18)

God expects us to follow His Word.

Compatibility does not mean that the couple likes everything the same. They do need some common interests, but many couples have vastly different likes and dislikes. This can become a discussion point and can actually make life more interesting. Some personalities, however, may tend to have more problems. When a couple is aware of their personality differences, it helps to avoid problems. Personality assessment, with tools such as the Taylor-Johnson Temperament Analysis or similar tools, can be helpful even for the pastoral level of counseling.

The couple must learn to argue in a way that they can resolve an issue. (See chapter 6, "The Ministry of the Marriage," on communication in marriage.) As the couple works on good communication and getting to know each other, the topic of sexuality needs to be covered.

Sex is very important, and God gives specific guidelines in 1 Corinthians 7:3–5:

> The husband should fulfill his marital duty to his wife, and likewise the wife to her husband. The wife's body does not belong to her alone but also to her husband. In the same way, the husband's body does not belong to him alone but also to his wife. Do not deprive each other except by mutual consent and for a time, so that you may devote yourselves to prayer.

Sex must not be the focal point. At some point in the marriage, sex may not be possible, due to illness or surgeries, but the relationship must go on. The couple must be willing to listen to each other and communicate well. This is why they need to practice communication before marriage— talking, laughing, enjoying time together, and discussing serious topics.

If the couple starts out with the mindset that there is an easy exit—a divorce—it becomes easier to go in that direction when the hard times come. They need to be encouraged before they marry that marriage is for a lifetime, through good times and bad, through sickness and health. They should plan to grow old together, which can be a joy and great comfort. Don't leave the door open for the option of splitting up; be determined to work through the hard times and enjoy the good times.

I was married the first time for forty-one years, a very good marriage before my wife passed. About a year or so later, I began to date, and it was very different for me. Instead of talking about having kids (not possible) or what a joyous time we would have together, we talked about what would happen if one of us became ill or incapacitated, had dementia, or needed care. We talked about who might die first and how the other would be cared for. We had to look at the hard stuff at the beginning. This was very helpful in making a full commitment to each other; we truly understood that we were not likely to enjoy even a few years before the real challenges would start.

Foundations are laid for the purpose of building a strong structure, where the wind and the waves have no effect on it. We make our foundation for our lives on the Word of God; likewise, marriage must be built on the same foundation.

> Therefore everyone who hears these words of mine and puts them into practice is like a wise man who built his house on the rock. The rain came down, the streams rose, and the winds blew and beat against that house; yet it did not fall, because it had its foundation on the rock. (Matthew 7:23)

6

The Ministry of Marriage

After a couple has prepared for marriage, they begin the marriage itself. The couple will need to continue the process of building the family on a strong foundation of the Word of God. With the roles well defined in the family system, they should consider the important relationships in that system, those of the husband and the wife.

To develop a good and functioning marriage relationship, we need to put in *energy*. This involves knowledge, understanding, love, and commitment. God has defined marriage as between a man and woman, and He intends for it to be for life, until death separates one from the other for a time. It is considered so important that he used marriage as an illustration of how we are to relate to Christ as His bride:

> I saw the Holy City, the new Jerusalem, coming down
> out of heaven from God, prepared as a bride beautifully
> dressed for her husband. (Revelation 21:2)

In order to maintain the marriage, we first must make sure our priorities are in line. These priorities should be as follows:

1. Jesus and you
2. Marriage
3. Children

4. Other family
5. Ministry
6. Work
7. Pleasure

We always seem to be working on these throughout life, so we might need to look at the list occasionally to make sure we are on track.

Unity or Oneness as a Goal

> For this reason, a man will leave his father and mother and be united to his wife, and the two will become one flesh. (Ephesians 5:31)

Larry Crabb, in his book *Marriage Builder*, talks about the unity or oneness we need to have in all three parts of the self. As humans, we are described as a *trichotomy*; that is, body, soul, and spirit. The body is the physical self; the soul is the mind—our real self, the part that lives on eternally while the body stays here; and the spirit connects us to God; it's the *imago dei*—God's image planted in each person.

God's Word states:

> May God himself, the God of peace, sanctify you through and through. May your whole spirit, soul and body be kept blameless at the coming of our Lord Jesus Christ. The one who calls you is faithful, and he will do it. (1 Thessalonians 5:23–24)

Body unity has to do with the sexual part or physical intimacy in the relationship. It is quite complex and does not mean only that we have sex together. Most can do that OK, but it may be difficult for some couples. Intimacy involves much more—it's having good communication, mutual respect, and understanding the kinds of things that make each other respond. Communication needs to be on a level that these issues can be discussed.

Intimacy involves words, physical touch, and communication about deep topics, feelings, respect, and honor.

A physical relationship is the act of sex, which is important but is not the only component in striving for unity. When the other parts of intimacy are in place, however, the physical act can be meaningful as well as full of pleasure. Being able to fully enjoy this together without shame or guilt builds love and respect and thus creates the body or physical unity.

Soul unity includes the following:

- Communication
- Mutual encouragement
- Sharing interests
- Working together
- Caring together (A healthy family system produces energy so that you can care for others together.)

One of the key parts of the relationship is communication. Poor communication—not making clear what one needs or wants, not being able to express feelings, saying the wrong things at the wrong time—can place a deep divide in the relationship.

Spirit unity is the spiritual part of the relationship—how we relate to God and each other on a spiritual level. This involves:

- Relationship with Christ
- Time together with the Lord
- Learning how to share needs and prayer concerns
- Devotional time
- Dedicated prayer time
- Keeping the evil out; knowing how to battle for your spiritual life

To keep our minds focused on Christ, Paul advises us to concentrate on the good things. To feed our spirits and souls, which also helps our bodies be healthier, we need to think on positive and wonderful themes:

> Finally, brothers and sisters, whatever is true, whatever
> is noble, whatever is right, whatever is pure, whatever is

lovely, whatever is admirable—if anything is excellent or praiseworthy—think about such things. (Philippians 4:8)

We must be on guard for this part of our lives. If temptation enters, we may draw away from our relationship with God, and then disunity begins and the relationship will suffer. We need to be always on our guard that spiritual unity is intact and keep refocusing ourselves on Christ.

Communication

Countless books have been written on the many communication styles. The most useful concepts for those in a pastoral counseling role are the following:

Types of Communication

- *Direct*: saying what we mean in a way that is meant to be understood
- *Metacommunication*: the meaning behind the words that are communicated, not being direct
- *Nonverbal*: communicating with body language, assent, dissent, disgust, pleasure, posturing, or movement of the head, arms, etc.

Styles of Communication

- *Casual*: maintains a normal state, joking, reporting what happened, telling stories describing something. This is a friendly basis; it's how friends and acquaintances might communicate. Neutral, nonconflict-generating, mostly friendly chatter.
- *Exploration*: intimate level, considering a theme in depth, explaining, speculating.
- *Direct speech*: being open, responsive, dedicated, sharing, listening, revealing oneself, using "I" phrases.
- *I feel … When you … (say, do, act,) speech*: allows us to express feelings without accusation or discounting the other.
- *Control speech*: used to change the mind of, manipulate, or control the other person, or to teach a concept.

The two categories of control speech are *light*, which would be teaching, directing, or persuading; and *heavy*, which would be blaming, presuming, insulting putting down, sarcasm, manipulating, or coercing.

The above styles and types of communication come from my own years of counseling and training families. Many authors have written of many other styles and types, but I have seen that these are the most useful in marital communication.

Rules for the Management of Conflicts in Marriage

(Adapted from Christian Medical Association Marriage Weekend 1994; used with permission)

1. Keep the Goal in Mind the Goal
   - Minister to the other in love.
   - Resolve the conflict.
   - Restore harmony.

2. Don't Play Counselor
   - Your mate can feel and think for himself or herself.
   - You cannot say, "I know what you are feeling, thinking" without asking.
   - You cannot presume you know what the other wants to say or interpret what they mean by what they just said.

3. Don't Play Archaeologist
   - If you have forgiven truly, the past will remain in the past.
   - Archaeologists dig for old bones from the past.
   - Dead bones need to stay in the past.

4. Speak of Only One Topic at a Time
   - If you must, make an agenda, and then stick to it.
   - Make sure you both are talking about the same thing!

Larry E. Banta, M.D.

If the conversation seems to be on many scattered issues, stop, regroup, and consider one thing at a time so that the goal of resolution can be attained, rather than just arguing.

5. You Must Respond Verbally to the Other Person
   - Don't ignore, turn your back, or pout.
   - Without words, you cannot resolve the problem.

6. Don't Use Insults
   - The purpose of insults is to injure.
   - The goal of the discussion is to resolve the problem.
   - Insults tend to detour us from the topic at hand.
   - We know *exactly* the insult that will hurt the other the most.

7. The Place and Time of the Discussion Is Negotiable
   - The expectation that the discussion must take place immediately is nothing more than an attempt to control rather than resolve.
   - It is better to make the invitation to talk about the theme at a particular time and place.

8. Know When to Suspend the Discussion
   - Suspend it when emotions get out of control.
   - Suspend it when you repeat yourselves and are not arriving at a solution.
   - Take a break and let emotions cool, but set a time to explore the topic again; agree to call a time-out before it gets hurtful.

Emotions are getting out of control when there is no longer discussion of the topic but the couple is just shooting words at each other. In counseling, I would tell couples it was like an Old West gunfight, ducking behind wagon and coming up just to shoot at each other. At that point, the couple is not making any progress toward the goal. If either of the couple feels overwhelmed or anxious, it is time to take a break.

Problems do not get resolved with the heart in control instead of the head.

9. You Can Disagree over Opinions or Facts but Not Both at the Same Time
    *   Allow the other the freedom to have his or her own opinion.
    *   Opinions are just opinions.
    *   Regarding facts, make sure you have all the facts and that they are accurate.
    *   Don't exaggerate or generalize.

If you are not sure of the facts, check them out before making assertions that may be designed to provoke the other into more arguing. Remember the goal of the conversation.

10. Eliminate the Words *Never* and *Always*
    *   *Never* and *always* are absolute words that have the purpose of provoking anger.
    *   These words discount your mate.
    *   These words distort facts and information.
    *   They contaminate the understanding that could lead to resolution.

Do not forget that the goal is to *resolve* the problem.

"In your anger do not sin": Do not let the sun go down while you are still angry. (Ephesians 4:26 NIV)

Patterns of Communication Centered in Christ

As the couple matures in the relationship, they must keep in mind the way that Jesus wants them to interact. Communication is more than just words; it involves action and investment of energy. Developing the following patterns takes time and practice. The husband and wife both need to take note of these patterns and redirect themselves to them to grow the relationship. The patterns of communication are as follows:

Caress: Recognize the value of the other; treat the other according to the *value* he or she has to you and with solicitude and consideration.

Listen: Active listening means investing the time to truly listen with the entire person responding. Do not think about other things while the other person is talking; do not interrupt; and comment without attacking. This is done because of the *value* the other has.

Initiate: Invest time and energy in the relationship, pitching in to get things done and to maintain things. Do not wait until something happens to do something.

Encourage: Believe in and desire the best for the other.

Resolve: Remember the goal of the interaction.

The goal of the discussion is always to restore harmony in the relationship, not to win the argument.

Minister: Ministering to the spouse means putting one's personal needs below those of the other. That is the concept of *sacrifice*.

In order to demonstrate love and sacrifice in the relationship, the following patterns of interacting are very helpful:

Request: Use polite language; don't demand but ask.

Forgive: We are all human and tend to fail. We need to recognize this in ourselves and our mates, forgiving and putting the past in the past. We need to express and accept the forgiveness.

Give: Because of the value of the other, give compliments, verbal caresses, special gifts, etc.

Share: Share your needs, feelings, dreams, friendship, pain, and joy. This is the goal of ministering to each other. We all have needs. Don't ignore them; share them.

Receive: Learn to receive from the other with gratitude. An attitude of gratitude honors God and your mate.

Love: Use active agape love in communication and action. Agape love refers to the kind of love God demonstrates in loving us unconditionally. God actively sent His Son to us. He did not just sit in heaven and think good thoughts about us.

Self-Centered Patterns of Communication

If we are concerned only about what we want to get out of the interaction and it is all about us, the following patterns might be a part of how we respond. Such patterns serve to destroy the other person, not build up him or her. These patterns do not help us to lovingly interact but serve to only win the argument and get our way. The couple needs to be encouraged to look out for these selfish patterns in themselves; they may need help in identifying them in a counseling situation:

- *Ignoring* what the other has to say
- *Interrupting* and not letting the other finish a thought
- *Demanding* our way; not compromising; not considering the other
- *Blocking* or *discouraging* by not letting the feelings of the other affect you; using degrading or negative words against the other
- *Arguing* only for the sake of arguing, not to resolve anything
- *Defending* our point of view, which is all that matters to us
- *Holding a grudge* and keeping count; keeping the anger inside and waiting for the moment you can use it against the other
- *Controlling* by not allowing the other to express his or her opinion
- *Rejecting* by throwing the words back and not allowing new ideas in (If it is not my way or my idea, it does not count.)
- *Condemning* by putting down the other for the ideas he or she may share, even to the point that he or she feels condemned by you (In this case, you might be assuming a divine role.)

Remember these scripture verses:

> Love is patient, love is kind. It does not envy, it does not boast, it is not proud. It does not dishonor others, it is not self-seeking, it is not easily angered, it keeps no record of wrongs. Love does not delight in evil but rejoices with the truth. It always protects, always trusts, always hopes, always perseveres. (1 Corinthians 13:4–7)

> You were taught, with regard to your former way of life, to put off your old self, which is being corrupted by its deceitful desires; to be made new in the attitude of your minds; and to put on the new self, created to be like God in true righteousness and holiness.
>
> Therefore, each of you must put off falsehood and speak truthfully to your neighbor, for we are all members

of one body. "In your anger do not sin": Do not let the sun go down while you are still angry, and do not give the devil a foothold. Anyone who has been stealing must steal no longer, but must work, doing something useful with their own hands, that they may have something to share with those in need.

Do not let any unwholesome talk come out of your mouths, but only what is helpful for building others up according to their needs, that it may benefit those who listen. And do not grieve the Holy Spirit of God, with whom you were sealed for the day of redemption. Get rid of all bitterness, rage and anger, brawling and slander, along with every form of malice. Be kind and compassionate to one another, forgiving each other, just as in Christ God forgave you. Follow God's example, therefore, as dearly loved children and walk in the way of love, just as Christ loved us and gave himself up for us as a fragrant offering and sacrifice to God. (Ephesians 4:22–5:2)

In Sickness and in Health until Death Do Us Part

Building the marriage on a strong foundation is fundamental. By learning the essentials of how to get along and practicing the best communication, respect, and mutual encouragement, we can be strong.

However, our enemy Satan is not pleased with the outcome and wants to drive us out of the safety of that foundation and make us unable to be effective or content. He wants to engage us in battle. We have to be prepared. The family is the stronghold of the church. If Satan can destroy the family, he is free to cause all kinds of damage. Are you ready for battle?

7

Ready for Battle?

In the foregoing chapters, we constructed a family system. We saw the various roles and the importance of the marriage relationship.

We are building on the firm foundation of the Word of God. That invites trouble—trouble from the enemy and even trouble from ourselves. We are imperfect, broken human beings, fully vulnerable to temptation and sometimes open to demonic influence, although we do well enough on our own in finding ways to disobey.

The moment we put on Christ, we must realize that we not only have joined God's kingdom but God's army, and we have joined in a spiritual battle. The battle belongs to the Lord, but we must be faithful to Him and stay close to Him so that we can live victoriously. There is the battle for our own souls and effectiveness. There are temptations and failures. The fact is that as we develop a strong family system, we are needed for the battle for the souls of others. We cannot live the Christian life in isolation. We are a community and must fight the battles together.

> Finally, be strong in the Lord and in his mighty power.
> Put on the full armor of God, so that you can take your
> stand against the devil's schemes. For our struggle is not
> against flesh and blood, but against the rulers, against
> the authorities, against the powers of this dark world and
> against the spiritual forces of evil in the heavenly realms.

Therefore, put on the full armor of God, so that when the day of evil comes, you may be able to stand your ground, and after you have done everything, to stand. (Ephesians 6:10–13)

It is easy to ignore the reality of the spiritual world and to go on with what we can see, feel, hear, and touch. The reality, however, is far different. One of the evil one's best tricks is to make us ignore the reality of his existence so that he can catch us off guard. We have to be aware of this but not look for a demon behind every door. Spiritual warfare has to do with how we battle against the forces of evil that have captivated many of our fellow human beings.

Given that there *is* a spiritual world, it may be necessary to reconsider what reality is and how it may change our perceptions.

What is reality? Do you believe in only whatever you experience with your five senses? There is more. Realize that you are not a body that has a soul; rather, *you are a soul that inhabits a body.* You are an eternal being, locked in time and space for a time.

Reality extends beyond the visible. The Bible describes an entire universe that we cannot comprehend. We easily accept the reality of the Holy Spirit, but we also must realize that evil spirits exist and interfere in our lives.

Fundamentally, nothing has changed since the time Jesus walked the earth. We have cars, electricity, and nicer houses, but people still sin. They are still in need of a Savior, and evil still resides on the earth. This is not the same world that God created when He said, "It is good." Something happened to the creation when Adam sinned.

We live in a corrupted, evil world in which Satan claims ownership. Satan's army is out to deceive and to cause us to deviate from following God.

The battle is spiritual.

The Spirit clearly says that in later times some will abandon the faith and follow deceiving spirits and things taught by demons. Such teachings come through hypocritical liars, whose consciences have been seared as with a hot iron. (1 Timothy 4:1–2)

The battle is against a kingdom.

> For our struggle is not against flesh and blood, but against
> the rulers, against the authorities, against the powers of
> this dark world and against the spiritual forces of evil in
> the heavenly realms. (Ephesians 6:12)

Satan is out for us!

> Your enemy the devil prowls around like a roaring lion
> looking for someone to devour. (1 Peter 5:8)

When Satan becomes directly involved in our lives, there may be demonic involvement; certain circumstances might lead to that. The danger signals that may put us in danger of demonization are as follows:

- Certain circumstances in growing up, particularly sexual abuse
- Religious orientation of family
- Experiences with the occult (Ouija boards, New Ageism, animism, Satanism, etc.)
- Involvement in a cult (spiritualism, animism, traditional religions such as Native Hawaiian or Santeria in Mexico and many others)
- Deliberate dealings with the devil
- Pornography, especially gay, child, bestial, extreme perversion

Some symptoms or signs of problems include:

- Lack of personal relationship with Christ (or having wandered away)
- Current temptations and difficulties
- New onset of or worsening mental health problems
- Addictions, especially methamphetamine, sexual, hallucinogens
- Voices in the head or outside (not related to a mental illness)
- Visions of evil characters
- Aversion to the Bible
- Discomfort in church

- Anger at the mention of the blood of Christ
- Raging at or cursing God
- Supernatural phenomena: seeing ghosts, things moving around without someone there, noises such as footsteps in the house when no one is walking about, a sense of evil in the home.

If this is an issue in your congregation, and the church leaders are not experienced in this type of battle, please find mature, knowledgeable Christians to assist with this. There is a good deal of risk if one is not prepared and does not know what he or she is doing.

When it appears that there is a problem of demonization—based on assessment by mature, knowledgeable Christian leaders—then there is a need for spiritual warfare to remove the demonic influence. One of the best guides I have found for dealing with spiritual warfare is Neal Anderson's *Bondage Breaker* (see bibliography), as well as other resources from him.

Consider the following with regard to temptation:

- We are in a spiritual battle.
- Though not all evil comes from demons, demons are real and active in the world today.
- Demonic activity will intensify as the end of the age approaches.
- We must be aware and ready to battle, when necessary.
- We must seek help from church leaders to deal with demons.
- We are all tempted in many ways but must seek ways to avoid temptation.
- If we are confronted with temptation, there is a way out. God is more powerful than the temptation. He will provide a way.

We cannot live in isolation. We need other believers, and we need to be involved in the ministry of the church in order to be best prepared for the battles that inevitably will confront us.

Because our battle is a spiritual battle, we must be aware of whatever is going on around us. Families need to be encouraged to take this very seriously. Temptations can take us by surprise. Satan is looking to deceive and destroy us. Our daily commission is to put on our armor. If we are not prepared for battle, we leave the door open for the enemy.

> Put on the full armor of God, so that you can take your stand against the devil's schemes. For our struggle is not against flesh and blood, but against the rulers, against the authorities, against the powers of this dark world and against the spiritual forces of evil in the heavenly realms. Therefore, put on the full armor of God, so that when the day of evil comes, you may be able to stand your ground, and after you have done everything, to stand. Stand firm then, with the belt of truth buckled around your waist, with the breastplate of righteousness in place, and with your feet fitted with the readiness that comes from the gospel of peace. In addition to all this, take up the shield of faith, with which you can extinguish all the flaming arrows of the evil one. Take the helmet of salvation and the sword of the Spirit, which is the word of God. And pray in the Spirit on all occasions with all kinds of prayers and requests. With this in mind, be alert and always keep on praying for all the Lord's people. (Ephesians 6:11–18)

8

Making Disciples: Raising the Children

We have developed a firm foundation by building on the unchanging Word of God. We have seen how to develop a good framework with a healthy family system and structure. We can see how to fulfill the scriptural roles of the man and woman and marriage within that structure. We are prepared to face the spiritual battles.

The next part of the system is the children. They are a blessing but can be a challenge, and we need energy and commitment to raise them properly.

God has a plan for each of us. Some couples are not able or have decided not to have children. Their journeys may be different, but they still are within God's plan, as he uses them in different ways. For them, it still is important to have structure in their homes and keep the marriage alive. Sometimes, not being able to have children may be very difficult for the couple, which may need to be addressed in counseling.

The Bible tells us of the blessing of having children:

> Children are a heritage from the LORD,
> offspring a reward from him.
> Like arrows in the hands of a warrior
> are children born in one's youth.

Blessed is the man
whose quiver is full of them.
They will not be put to shame
when they contend with their opponents in court. (Psalm
127:3–5)

The Bible gives us God's plan for raising children. Many scripture verses deal with this important ministry. There are duties of the children and duties of the parents. Our approaches can work much better if we follow God's guidelines.

Children, obey your parents in the Lord, for this is right. "Honor your father and mother"—which is the first commandment with a promise— "so that it may go well with you and that you may enjoy long life on the earth."

Fathers, do not exasperate your children; instead, bring them up in the training and instruction of the Lord. (Ephesians 6:1–4)

To be effective, the home needs to have structure, as was outlined previously. Having rules and consequences, with strong leadership from the parents, will serve to strengthen the structure of the home. It is not a rigid structure; it has flexibility, and it needs to allow for changes as the children grow up and get ready to be out on their own.

Our objective is to love and nurture our children and raise them up to know Christ and to love Him so that they can be productive, mature Christian adults.

As you may recall from chapter 2, structure in the home consists of:

- Discipline
- Scheduling
- Rituals
- Boundaries
- Hierarchy
- Roles and responsibilities

Within that structure, we will do our best as parents to keep children on track. Children, however, do present some challenges. One of the important challenges for us, as parents, is addressing children's behaviors so that we can guide them into well-grounded, adult Christians.

All children will present some type of challenging behavior. The problem is that we are born with a sin nature; we all tend toward doing the wrong things, disobeying, and testing the limits. As parents, understanding those behaviors can help us design a good approach. If we are unaware of what we are doing or don't think about it, we may allow too much to go by, ignoring the challenging behaviors, and the child will not learn. The concept of discipline, discussed earlier, can help us approach these issues in the best way possible.

Passive parenting is the practice of letting children grow up on their own—not paying attention to their behaviors, not addressing right or wrong, and letting them determine for themselves what is good. This never works. As parents, we must put energy into the system by noticing behaviors and addressing them in the best way possible.

To gain an *understanding* of behavior, rather than looking at the behavior alone, it helps to see the whole picture. All behavior has a purpose. The child is generally trying to communicate something, test something, or provoke something. Sometimes, it may be a product of a mental illness or may contribute to it. Our response to the behavior may serve to increase the behavior, decrease it, or extinguish it altogether. Our own attitudes and reactions to the child may unknowingly promote significant behaviors. We parents need to be aware of what we are doing.

The way we respond to behaviors may encourage or reinforce the behavior, or it may discourage the behavior, which is *negative reinforcement*. The concept of negative reinforcement is designed to produce some sort of pain or discomfort to discourage the behaviors but never in an abusive way. It's always meant to have the goal of *teaching* the child.

We must have proper discipline, designed to teach and not destroy the child; this is very important to helping him or her learn the proper behaviors—what is right or wrong. This sets the foundation for their spiritual development, helping them along the way to become disciples of Jesus.

Not all behavior is bad; it is merely what we do in a particular circumstance. We want to promote the good and extinguish or lessen the bad so that a good moral framework is developed. We also need to take care not to allow the behavior to define who the child is but to unconditionally love the child, apart from the behaviors. This requires us to exercise the forgiveness we are capable of as followers of Christ.

One of the best ways to teach good behavior is to model it in ourselves. It is evident in the way we live and the values we promote. We constantly teach by our actions.

We also influence behaviors through reinforcement, by applying a consequence that either promotes or discourages a particular behavior. Three types of reinforcement are as follows:

1. *Negative reinforcement*—that which serves to discourage, *not* reinforce, the behavior
2. *Positive reinforcement*—that which serves to promote desired behaviors
3. *Unintentional reinforcement*—that which we do unintentionally that may serve to reinforce or discourage desired or undesired behaviors

Behaviors can also be extinguished if ignored—that is, paying no attention to them—but this must be used judiciously, as certain behaviors may escalate to a level that needs a consequence applied.

Negative Reinforcement

Do not let the word *negative* give you the idea that this is something bad; it just means that we do *not* reinforce the behavior. Some types of negative reinforcement are considered abusive or are designed to cause harm, rather than maintaining the goal of teaching what is proper and good and to maintain love and acceptance for the child. These would be cruel punishment or withdrawal of love from the child.

Most approaches, however, are quite appropriate and helpful. Positive reinforcement promotes the behavior. Negative reinforcement, though necessary, needs to be done with love and a bit of flexibility so as not to overwhelm children with the consequences. It is very important for the parent not to act impulsively or with anger but to take time to consider and to make the consequence fit the bad behavior. The parent needs to be humble and aware to see if the consequence may have provoked worse behavior; if so, the approach needs to be modified.

- *Discipline*: Negative consequences are designed to teach. Discipline might include some discomfort and loss of freedom, but it has an aspect of providing information that promotes appropriate behavior. Grounding or a time-out are often helpful measures of discipline.
- *Natural consequences*: An example is a child who is told not to run on the loose gravel, as she will get hurt, but she does, and so she gets hurt. Sometimes this, plus words to associate the natural consequence with the behavior, might be sufficient to provide the necessary lesson.
- *Verbal correction*: Properly applied, verbal correction can provide an effective impact. Words that are too harsh, long-winded, or delivered from loss of control by the parent might have the opposite effect, promoting the undesired behavior.
- *Punishment*: Generally not designed to teach, punishment might consist of inflicting some type of discomfort, severe restrictions, or—for children who are out of control—sometimes confinement in a juvenile facility to get their attention and draw them back on track. Corporal punishment, properly applied, is effective, but it is so often misused that it can be punishment, as defined here, or even abuse, rather than discipline that is designed to teach and encourage proper behavior. This is sometimes needed in order to get children's attention so they can respond to the normal discipline and teaching.
- *Time out*: This means time out from attention. It can be very effective, if properly applied for the defined behaviors.

Time-Out Procedure

- Define a few behaviors to work with, such as defiance, talking back, disobedience, fighting, and so forth.

- Find a boring corner and a chair for the child to sit during the time-out, and try to use this spot consistently, if possible.
- Explain the process to the child. This is best done when not responding to a behavior. "This is what we are going to do when you [define the unwanted behaviors], and this is how we will do it. I will use the timer. If you complain or cry, the timer restarts each time. When you are quiet for [x] minutes, you will be allowed to get up."
- Use the same process each time.
- When behavior occurs, say, "You have done what we've asked you not to do, and so you are going to time-out." No other words are spoken. Ignore the child's protestations; do not respond to them.
- If the child will not go willingly, help him to the chair. If he refuses to go, other consequences might be needed.
- Use one minute per year of age; for example, a three-year-old sits for three minutes. Time out is not usually helpful for those over ten years of age.
- Using some type of timing device—kitchen timer, watch, or stopwatch—start the time when the child is sitting quietly. If the protests begin or the child says something, restart the clock without saying a word. The time is complete if the child sits quietly for the designated time.
- At the end of the prescribed time, the child is released. If there is no damage to clean up, then give just a word or two about improving his behavior and let him go. No lengthy discussions are needed, as he already has completed the consequence.

Grounding is a process of removing established privileges that are important to the child so as to mold the identified behavior to be more appropriate.

Grounding Procedure

- Within the structure of the family, there must be privileges that can be earned or lost due to behaviors. Grounding implies loss of one or more privileges.
- Decide for which behaviors you would use grounding with the particular child.

- Find out which privilege seems important to the child.
- Decide on a specific length of time that is reasonable and clearly understood to both parties.

Let's say your teenager has acted disrespectfully to you. You might "ground" him or her from using the phone or social media for two weeks (although you might want to say six months or ten years!). After maybe ten days of good behavior, you might provide some relief, reducing or eliminating the restrictions as a positive reinforcement.

When grounding the child, you might offer ways for the child to reduce the time, such as special chores or writing assignments—be creative—but you might want to avoid telling the child of the potential reduction and instead, provide it as a surprise when assigned tasks are completed and behavior is more appropriate. This turns it into more of a positive experience. The consequence might be fourteen days of grounding, and at the successful completion of ten days, you might advise the child that he or she has done well, and if he or she can continue for one more day, then the grounding is over (or if certain assignments or work is completed, then he or she is free).

We must avoid expressing anything that the child might interpret as an indication that our love is conditional.

In applying negative consequences, the parent needs to take care not to withdraw love from the child, whatever the child might be guilty of. We can hate the behavior but not the child, the same as we would hate the sin and love the sinner. It is easy to say or do certain things that reflect the idea that the parent hates the child. This can be interpreted as rejection and may further intensify the conflict between the parent and child.

Positive Reinforcement

In order to maintain a healthy environment in the home, it is important to concentrate on the use of positive approaches as much as possible but not to neglect negative reinforcement-related consequences when it is necessary to redirect unwanted behaviors. Everything, however, is done in love, following the guidelines given us in the scriptures:

Fathers do not embitter your children, or they will become discouraged. (Colossians 3:21 NIV)

Basic Guidelines

Positive approaches, when applied properly, are the most potent in promoting behavior change. We must be careful, however, with children who have come from negative backgrounds—suffering from physical abuse or verbal abuse; feeling that they never could please the alcoholic parent; younger children on the street who were low in the hierarchy and whose superiors constantly degraded them. These children often are sensitive to positive reinforcement, so the initial dose cannot be high. Pay attention to the power in your words (see *Words of praise* point, below, in "Positive Reinforcement Approaches"). A child from this background might have finally done something well, so the parent uses high-powered words but then later finds the child in her room, with everything torn apart, crying on her bed. She had an overdose of positive reinforcement and could not handle it.

Another rule with positive reinforcements is the power of the nonverbal reward. We do not want to provide a high-powered reward for a small positive behavior. We need to carefully consider the value of the reward, as well as the words of praise, so that it is appropriate to the level of good behavior.

Positive Reinforcement Approaches

- *Rewards*: For children who are learning to attach, the most powerful rewards are those with a human component. Nonetheless, material rewards are powerful for reinforcing a job well done, appropriate behaviors, or having done something especially good or thoughtful.
- *Special privileges*: Choose a privilege that is out of the ordinary, one that might be earned by some special achievement or good schoolwork. This could include such things as staying up a bit later on a nonschool night or spending time with friends outside the home. Creativity is helpful here as well.
- *Words of praise*: Praise for a job well done comes in a variety of strengths, or *valences*. If we say, "Good job" or "Job well done," it is positive but of low valence. "Very good" is a bit higher, while

"excellent" is higher still. "Fantastic, unbelievable, wow!" is probably the ultimate and is reserved for very special occasions for the older child or for the younger child who can tolerate high praise without side effects, such as anxiety, becoming overwhelmed, engaging in destructive behaviors, or going into a rage.

- *Monetary allowance*: Within many cultures, the provision of a weekly monetary reward is helpful, at least in learning how to handle money but also in providing the caregiver something to take away, if the behavior warrants, or to give the child the opportunity to earn more, as good behaviors warrant. The amount can be small but enough to buy some inexpensive personal items when going to the store. Some families will not be able to afford this, but you could use some other system in which points are earned toward some special time or reward.

- *Special time with parent(s)*: This can be a very powerful reward. It might be a trip to the store or ice cream shop, but it could be something such as a meal out or a movie, depending on the behavior that is being rewarded.

- *"Catching" the child in good behavior*: This takes a bit of energy on the parent's part, but it is powerful. During the course of the day, you may notice a couple of your children playing well together, sharing, or getting along with each other. You can approach them, make brief eye contact, place a hand on the shoulder of each child, and say a few positive words (e.g., "I really like the way you are playing together today"; "I appreciate that you are getting along"). These phrases connect the parent to the children in a positive way, as you are expressing appreciation for them. A few carefully planted words of affection can be helpful as well: "We are so proud of you," or "We really enjoy being with you." Do not overdo it, but a few sincere moments like this are very powerful.

- *Star chart*: This system works with younger children, ages four through ten or eleven (maybe older if the child is developmentally delayed). Make a chart with the days of the week along the top and with the behaviors that need to be promoted or discouraged listed on the side. Place a star for each day that the goal is met for the behavior. After the child earns a predetermined number of stars, an initial reward of low value is given; this increases as the stars accumulate. When an unwanted behavior is no longer a problem, it is removed from the list to make room for another problem behavior or desirable behaviors. (See sample chart, below.) Charts easily can be made on a computer or by hand. Stars can be drawn in, or you can use stickers. If possible, the child can place the star in the appropriate column when a task is completed.

	Monday	Tuesday	Wednesday	Thursday	Friday	Saturday	Sunday
Clean Room		★			★		
Chores			★				
Obey						★	
No Swear Words							★

Passing Along the Faith

George Barna's book *Transforming Our Children into Spiritual Champions* offers the statistic that those people who are reached with the message of Jesus before the age of twelve are much more likely to remain involved in the church throughout their entire lifetimes, following God's Word (see bibliography).

Family as a Ministry

- The role of both the man and the woman is to minister to each other in the name of Jesus and then to minister to the children
- Family life is a ministry for all of us, and we must make it a priority.
- Our primary job is to pass along the faith to our children while remaining strong ourselves.

First Steps

Priority One: My Relationship with Christ

Parenting as a Christian is a ministry, the most important one of all. When we are on a mission, we develop a mission statement so that our purpose and activities lead to a beneficial result. It is helpful to have a mission statement to guide us on our earthly journey for whatever we might be doing, including ministering to our own family.

My mission statement—I am here to:

- design a focus for family ministry and put the mission statement into action;
- walk the talk, and talk the walk; and
- live and work as a servant of the most high God.

The family mission statement may be something like, "We will raise our children to become productive, mature, committed adult Christians." We might also have a mission statement for work and for our own outside ministry with the church. Pastors especially need to have a mission statement to keep the focus on what is important.

Walking the Talk

Walking with God takes a great deal of energy. We must demonstrate our faith through action and not just words. Teaching is a way of life—we are always teaching something—and all that we do is an example. We must do the following:

- Live out the Word in a way that others will notice.
- Admit our mistakes when we are wrong.
- Seek forgiveness.
- Forgive others.
- Demonstrate compassion and care for others.
- Love the unlovely, showing unconditional love in our interactions with others.

- Give generously.
- Maintain a positive attitude.
- Show humility.
- Show reverence for the holy.
- Refrain from gossip.
- Demonstrate our priorities.
- Practice active listening.

All of the above are examples of *love in action.*

In order to walk the talk, it is necessary to put energy into it, have a purpose, and mold our behavior to that which God desires so we can represent Him and be His hands and feet in our families and our world.

As parents, we constantly are teaching something, so we need to be aware of what we are teaching and make those lessons purposeful. In being aware of how we act and what we do daily, we can then see what we are teaching our children and those around us. If we are kind to a stranger, reach out to help someone, or treat those around us with godly love and kindness, it will be passed on to our children and others.

Everything we do is an example of what we believe and what we treasure. We are going to make mistakes, so we must be humble, admit our mistakes, and seek forgiveness and reconciliation.

The children will see that the parents give of themselves and their finances to help the church and others, and they will want to follow that as the action of love we are teaching.

How do the parents represent their relationship with God? Do they hold Him in high regard and recognize and treat the holy with respect? For example, when there is a communion service, baptism, or worship time, they must hold that as a high priority in their lives. Parents should not use God's name in vain. They need to speak reverently of Him and live in gratitude, recognizing that He is their provider.

Listening to each other as a couple and to the children with active listening and full attention and responding with respect is a way to teach children how to listen and how to demonstrate love in action.

Living as representatives of Christ for the family and as pastors or church leaders and encouraging others to do this is a very important task. Each one shows by his or her behavior what it means to live for Christ. This means being humble, admitting one's mistakes, and seeking forgiveness from a spouse or a child, if appropriate. They must show love in an active way to those around them so there is no doubt that they are different. They live a different life than that of the world.

Talking the Walk

Living by example and demonstrating what it is to live, work, and parent as a committed Christian is a very important step. It also is important, however, that parents are able to explain and talk about what it means to live and serve the high King of heaven and our Lord and Savior.

The Bible gives us guidelines on how Christians should promote God's Word and love by actively teaching.

> You are the salt of the earth. But if the salt loses its saltiness, how can it be made salty again? It is no longer good for anything, except to be thrown out and trampled underfoot.
>
> You are the light of the world. A town built on a hill cannot be hidden. Neither do people light a lamp and put it under a bowl. Instead, they put it on its stand, and it gives light to everyone in the house. In the same way, let your light shine before others, that they may see your good deeds and glorify your Father in heaven. (Matthew 5:13–16)

> These are the commands, decrees and laws the LORD your God directed me to teach you to observe in the land that you are crossing the Jordan to possess, so that you, your children and their children after them may fear the LORD your God as long as you live by keeping all his decrees and commands that I give you, and so that you may enjoy long life. Hear, Israel, and be careful to obey so that it may go well with you and that you may increase greatly in a land flowing with milk and honey, just as the LORD, the God of your ancestors, promised you.

> Hear, O Israel: The LORD our God, the LORD is one. Love the LORD your God with all your heart and with all your soul and with all your strength. These commandments that I give you today are to be on your hearts. Impress them on your children. Talk about them when you sit at home and when you walk along the road, when you lie down and when you get up. Tie them as symbols on your hands and bind them on your foreheads. Write them on the doorframes of your houses and on your gates. (Deuteronomy 6:1–9)

A famous university professor, a teacher of teachers, started his class with the usual educational material during the first week. At the beginning of the second week, he asked his students, "What did you teach last week?"

The students were a bit confused and replied, "We have only just begun to learn to teach. How can we be teaching?"

The professor then explained that we are always teaching something to someone by our attitude and behaviors. We may condone or reject certain ideas; we may show anger appropriately or inappropriately; we may sit and talk with others and share ideas.

We are *always teaching something*. The teacher teaches in all circumstances, and we are all teachers. What are you teaching the children?

Find moments throughout each day in which something can be taught. Know the facts, stay in the Word, and keep yourself close to the Savior

Discipline is an opportunity to show love and to teach what Jesus would want in the situation. Use words to encourage, uplift, express care and concern, express love, correct, instruct, calm, uplift Jesus, and share your life with the child.

> But the wisdom that comes from heaven is first of all pure; then peace-loving, considerate, submissive, full of mercy and good fruit, impartial and sincere. Peacemakers who sow in peace raise a harvest of righteousness. (James 3:17–18)

Finding the teachable moments is one of the great challenges of parenting or in our interactions with others. Children may exhibit undesirable behavior, for which a consequence is necessary. Discussion thereafter can be a teachable moment. During mealtimes or devotion times, questions can come up—hopefully, they will.

In raising my own children, I once heard, "I don't think I believe in God anymore." That challenge led to a lively discussion about creation and evolution, not condemnation. This was a time we listened to their concerns and then discussed the rationale of our belief.

Walking in nature and finding an interesting bug or animal and discussing the wonders of creation can be another opportunity. Times of stress for adolescents—with the usual breakups and trials and tribulations—can be golden moments to share love and concern, as well as guidance for living.

I recall the words my father said during our times together, just the two of us in the car, and I still carry those words of wisdom with me. Take advantage of those little moments to make a difference, and recognize that these can be impactful moments.

When parents effectively demonstrate Christ in their *walk* and *talk*, quite often their children are then ready to receive Christ as their Savior. When children come to the point that they understand sin and know that they need a Savior and are ready to come to Him, we need to know what to do.

Every Christian parent needs to know how to bring their children to Christ; the church's job is to teach them how to do it.

Lead children to faith in Christ by explaining the plan of salvation when children are ready to understand. Pray with them and lead them in the steps to accepting the Lord.

It is a wonderful scene when a child is baptized by a parent!

The hopeful outcome of our efforts of demonstrating our faith is that children will want to accept Jesus as their personal Savior. This is a personal decision; it's one that cannot be forced. It must be taken seriously, and appropriate steps should be taken when children are ready.

A useful guide for this is found at https://www.teachkids.eu/pdfs/ucan_lead.pdf. This is a PDF file of a book called *U-can Lead Children to Christ* by Dr. Sam Doherty.

Another helpful source is the website called the Roman Road to Salvation, from Teen Missions International, at https://teenmissions.org/roman-road-to-salvation. (See the bibliography at the end of this book.)

Follow the ABCs for the basics:

The child must be able to (A) acknowledge that he or she is a sinner, (B) believe that Jesus died, rose again, and has paid for our sins, and (C) confess that Jesus is Lord and so accept Him as his or her personal Lord and Savior.

Here are some suggested verses:

Acknowledge

> For all have sinned and fall short of the glory of God. (Romans 3:23)

> For the wages of sin is death, but the gift of God is eternal life in Christ Jesus our Lord. (Romans 6:23)

Believe

> They replied, "Believe in the Lord Jesus, and you will be saved—you and your household. (Acts 16:31)

> Consequently, faith comes from hearing the message, and the message is heard through the word about Christ. (Romans 10:17)

Confess

> If you declare with your mouth, "Jesus is Lord," and believe in your heart that God raised him from the dead, you will be saved. For it is with your heart that you believe and are justified, and it is with your mouth that you profess your faith and are saved. As Scripture says, "Anyone who believes in him will never be put to shame." (Romans 10:9–11)

Consequently, faith comes from hearing the message, and the message is heard through the Word about Christ.

> Peter replied, "Repent and be baptized, every one of you, in the name of Jesus Christ for the forgiveness of your sins. And you will receive the gift of the Holy Spirit. The promise is for you and your children and for all who are far off—for all whom the Lord our God will call." (Acts 2:38–39)

Once the child has prayed to receive the Lord, the scripture states that the believer's baptism is the next step.

Now the journey is only beginning. With the gift of the Holy Spirit, the child has more power to resist temptation and do those things that please and glorify God.

To effectively make disciples—Jesus's followers—of our children, we must:

- Pass along the faith.
- Walk the talk.
- Talk the walk.
- Live the Word.
- Maintain ourselves as salt and light in this dark world.

9

Sexuality Education
in the Home

This chapter can be used to develop materials that a church might use to help parents provide the necessary information in a biblical framework. It also may be used by youth leaders to provide the education when the children have reached an age when it is appropriate. It is vital that the children be trained in order to undo what the world is already teaching them.

In the normal Christian home, it is the parents' job to provide sexuality education for their preadolescent children. As the world is the main teacher of this topic, our children are bombarded with false and misleading information without moral foundation. It is, therefore, even more vital that our children are provided with the correct information and the opportunity to decide to live sexually pure lives. The ages at which this information can be best learned (and not cause more problems) are around age eleven for girls and age twelve for boys. This is generally the time when the body is just beginning to change for both girls and boys.

In our world, however, sexuality is promoted at all ages so we must provide age-appropriate education as the child can manage it. This includes privacy while dressing and answering questions about the differences between boys and girls that each might ask. There may also be questions about gender.

As mentioned previously in regard to our foundation in Christ, the world does not have that foundation, so anything is permissible that one decides is OK. There is great pressure on children in several mostly developed countries to decide that they are not what God designed them to be. Boys start thinking they want to be girls, or girls want to be boys. Children are easily confused and can be convinced by passive parents and peers that it is OK *not* to be their assigned gender. This must be handled in a firm, noncritical manner, explaining that God created male and female; no error was made.

We must model our gender-appropriate behaviors as mother and father, inspiring interests in those things that better define one or the other but not discouraging interests in some things that the other gender does, explaining this does not define who we are. Many girls make fine mechanics, and boys can be great ballet dancers. Our interests or careers do not determine that we might be in the wrong body. Getting a handle on this early might prevent later confusion and the serious emotional problems that may accompany a decision to try to change to the other gender.

More detailed and in-depth sexuality information can be provided in a variety of ways but should roughly follow the outline provided here, so as to cover all the important aspects. It can be done in five sessions. (This will be further elaborated to allow your own development of the appropriate curriculum.)

The sessions need to be constructed in such a way that the parents explain most of it. It can effectively be done with the same-sex parent taking the child somewhere private to spend time talking about the subjects noted below. It also can be explained by the church youth group, separately for boys and girls, over a several-week period; this might involve Christian professionals who provide good information. If the church does not provide the proper information, it is imperative that the parents provide it. The five sessions are as follows:

1. Anatomy and the Developing Body
2. The Sexual Act
3. Sex and the Bible
4. Consequences of Disobedience
5. Commitment to Sexual Purity

1. Anatomy and the Developing Body

This session needs to include diagrams and drawings, which can be obtained from the internet or other sources. The diagrams should show the process of physical development and the changes that occur throughout puberty. The proper names for each part of the anatomy must be provided, which will help correct those who know the common vulgar terms. One source of information is www.intoxicatedonlife.com. This website has good resources and diagrams.

For the girls, spend a bit more time explaining menses and what happens to their bodies each month. Allow them to feel comfortable enough to ask questions. The boys will not need quite as many details regarding menstruation (such as feminine hygiene), but they do need to understand the process.

Once the anatomy is explained, along with the changes that happen to their bodies, have a few words about modesty and physical boundaries, as well as appropriate and inappropriate touch.

2. The Sexual Act

This session can be rather short and to the point, so as not to produce arousal but to explain things in a matter-of-fact way. The vocabulary needed includes *arousal, ejaculation,* and *orgasm.* A short explanation and brief description of each is sufficient. After that is done, follow the sperm to the egg with the help of diagrams to explain what happens to produce the new life. Information at this point needs to include that as soon as the sperm makes it into the ova, the new life is a person and will become an adult someday, if all goes well. Briefly trace the development of the baby in the context of the wonderful complexities of God's new creation. At this point, there may be questions about abortion, if they were taught about it in school. They must understand that this is a human being, and we have no right to take that life away. Whenever possible, remind children of the spiritual aspects of a loving sexual relationship.

3. Sex and the Bible

This session can be very interesting and fun, as well as informative. One way to do it in a youth group format is a "Sword Drill." Everyone brings a Bible to class. Verses are assigned to each one to read and to make a short commentary. (The verses can be found in any Bible; many have indexes or concordances. Other references can be useful, such as *Nave's Topical Bible*.) The instructor will cover topics of marriage, lust, adultery, fornication, and other areas that are pertinent, being sure to cover important passages, such as those that address issues concerning married life found in 1 Corinthians 7.

If done in the home, find and read the pertinent passages and discuss the consequences of sin in this area of our lives.

There are many more but here are some suggested verses:

1. Genesis 1:27 (the only genders are male and female)
2. Genesis 2:23–24 (man instructed on leaving parents and cleaving to wife)
3. Matthew 5:31–32; 19:3–12; Mark 10:2; Luke 16:18; 1 Corinthians 7:10–17 (concerning divorce)
4. Matthew 5:28; Mark 4:19; John 8:44; 1 Corinthians 9:27; 10:6–7; Ephesians 4:22; 1 Titus 6:9; 2 Titus 2:22; 4:3–4; Titus 2:12; James 1:14–15; 4:1–3; 1 Peter 2:11; 4:3; 2 Peter 2:18; 3:3; 1 John 2:16–17; Jude 1, 18 (concerning lust)
5. Matthew 5:28, 32; 15:19; 19:9; Mark 7:21; 10:11–12, 19; Luke 16:18; Acts 15:20, 29; Romans 1:28–29, 32; 7:3; 1 Corinthians 5:9–10; 6:15–18; 10:8; 2 Corinthians 12:21; Galatians 5:19, 21; 1 Titus 1:9–10; 2 Titus 3:6; James 2:11; 1 Peter 4:3–4; 2 Peter 2:9–10, 14; Jude 1 (adultery)
6. 1 Corinthians 6:9–10, 13, 15–18; 9:27; 2 Corinthians 12:21; Galatians 5:19–21; Ephesians 4:17–19; 5:5; Colossians 3:5; 1 Thessalonians 4:5; 2 Titus 3:6; 1 Peter 4:2–3 (fornication, sensuality)
7. 1 Corinthians 7 (marriage)

4. Consequences to Disobedience

This is another session that could benefit from the input of a health professional if done in a youth group. The consequences of sex outside of marriage need to be discussed, including the possibility of pregnancy, AIDS and other sexually transmitted diseases, and psychological effects (adultery, marital breakup, consequences of sex before marriage). The facts must be presented clearly and concisely so that children understand there is danger outside of God's plan.

5. Commitment to Sexual Purity

After all is said and done, the child can take time to consider the benefits of following God's direction and understanding His plan for sexuality in the context of a healthy God-centered marriage. Some parents incorporate a special dedication prayer; some invite children to sign special pledges; some have cards made with the promise and a place for the child's signature. Others have found that the use of symbolic jewelry commemorating the pledge makes it meaningful—a necklace for the girls with a designed key, for example. This key can be presented to the husband on the wedding night, symbolizing the sharing of their love together. Nowadays, the boys might like something similar.

10

Ready to Launch?

Preparing a teen to leave home and accept responsibility for his or her own upkeep requires a number of skills that are normally acquired in a typical family home. At about eighteen to twenty-one years of age, he or she is ready to launch, to get out in life mostly on one's own. Some are more prepared than others, even in a normal home. In a healthy family system, they will have support as they go out.

The process must be started during the teen years, with the adolescent and the parents working together through the list of skills that need to be established so that a successful transition can occur. This can be an exciting time, yet they may be filled with anxiety. Some kids do not want to leave due to fear of failure on the outside. This protocol can help to reduce some of the anxiety.

Getting out on their own requires that children be *able* to live on their own. Be realistic. If there are problems in development, intellect, mental health, or physical health that might make it more difficult, you need to recognize this as you consider the following list of skills needed to make the transition. It's important and helpful to work on conquering as many of the necessary skills as possible for those unable to make the transition to independent living. If the young adult is not able to acquire all the skills, it might be necessary for the him or her to stay at home for a while, or he or she may need services (provided in some countries) to help him or her to be as independent as possible.

The necessary skills are as follows:

1. Getting Ready to Go

    —Setting expectations
    —Leaving in a good way
    —Changing relationships but not being cut off
    —Adjusting to the idea of life away from home

Preparing the way starts in early adolescence with casual talk about what children want to do when they are grown—what kind of job they'll have, their living arrangements, etc. Offering little hints to them along the way (e.g., "You might need to know about this when you are on your own") can be very helpful in raising the necessary questions. It is then a natural part of conversation as time grows nearer for him or her to take on adult responsibilities and living on one's own. If children maintain a good relationship with their parents, the transition will be much more likely to be successful. It can be risky for them to leave without the support of parents or if they are not ready.

2. Personal Hygiene; Taking Care of the Body

    —Daily self-care, showering, brushing teeth, use of deodorant, shaving
      * Understanding normal body functions
      * Knowing when to seek medical help
    —First aid knowledge
      * Proper exercise

Personal care allows the adolescent to feel more confident and better able to face the world. Looking good, smelling good, and being in good shape all contribute to a sense of well-being and responsibility. Adolescents should learn basic first aid and how to seek medical help, including how to get insurance and where to go when they are ill, as well as how to take care of minor illnesses, such as a cough or a cold, diarrhea, or stomach upset that doesn't need an emergency visit to the hospital or doctor. Much of this is provided in most schools, if the child is able to attend. A reliable online resource is www.webmd.com.

3. Nutrition
   —A balanced diet
      * Buying groceries
   —Preparing and storing food, including basic cooking skills

A good start for children, early in life, is to help out in the kitchen with Mother or Father as food is prepared and to learn how to safely manage the utensils used to prepare and store food properly.

In some cultures, learning to hunt and fish, usually with the father, and preparing the game meat is a task mostly for boys but sometimes girls get to learn that as well.

If you live near stores, knowing how to manage money and purchase the necessary items is an important skill.

A resource that provides simple directions for a balanced diet is www.healthline.com. A food-budget calculator can be found at https://spendsmart.extension.iastate.edu/plan/what-you-spend.

4. Caring for Clothing

   —Buying adequate clothing
   —Proper washing, drying, folding, storing, dry cleaning, and ironing
   —Dressing appropriately

Most cultures make use of clothing so this task must be learned. It's important for children to have the basic knowledge of purchasing clothing within an acceptable budget and making sure they have the right clothing for the right climate and weather conditions. Most children in their early teen years can acquire the skill of washing and caring for their clothing.

5. Money and Finances

   —Understanding the financial system
      * Bank accounts and use of checks, credit cards, and keeping track of the money
   —Proper basic budgeting skills

Management of money is one of the issues that can break up a marriage and lead to frustration and difficulties in life. Learning how to manage finances is very important; it is also important not to live beyond what you can afford. With the advanced technologies, it is easy to buy the latest gadget, phone, tablet, etc., even when it does not fit in the budget. Credit cards and easy loans can make for major disasters in the near future. It is helpful to start out children with an allowance, even a small amount, that is earned through work around the home. Two excellent resources are crown.org, and ramseysolutions.com. Both are helpful in developing sound financial management, starting when children are very young.

6. Taking Care of Your Home

   —Appliances
   —Care of the kitchen
   —Carpet and floor care
   —Bathroom care
   —Bedroom care
       * Making the bed
       * Keeping dirty clothes in one place and clean clothes in another
   —Outdoor maintenance
       * Caring for yard, landscaping
       * Keeping space clean

No matter what type of home your child may live in, there are always things to learn about how to keep it clean and healthy. The home must be kept clean and safe for the occupants to have a comfortable environment.

7. Transportation

   —Public transportation, how to use it
       * Purchasing and maintaining a vehicle (car, bicycle, motorcycle)
       * Appropriate driving skills and licensing (car and driver), as well as insurance

Learning how to get from one point to another is important, even if you live in a rural area far from the city. It may not be necessary to have a vehicle, depending on the circumstances, but it is necessary to know how to use the buses and other forms of transport to get where you need to go.

8. Spiritual Skills

—Daily time with God, Bible reading, and prayer
—Finding a church
—Developing good spiritual habits

In chapter 8, "Making Disciples: Raising the Children," there are some methods that can help parents to develop spiritual habits in their children so that they will not leave the faith when they leave home and so they will know that their faith is their own, not just what the parents or peers want them to follow. Wherever children end up, they will know to keep up with Bible reading and prayer, as well as meeting together with other believers to strengthen each other so as to be salt and light in a dark world and to pass the faith along to their own children.

9. Leisure Skills

—Wisely using free time without overspending
—Developing healthy habits of exercise and hobbies
  * Maintaining the sporting skills developed in the growing-up years.

These habits are often passed on by example. There are many ways to relax, even in remote areas. Learning how to relax and restore energy is vital. Life is better if we can learn to play as well as to work and then keep the two in balance

10. Job-Related Skills

—Looking for work
—Interviewing, writing a résumé, filling out applications
—Obtaining and maintaining employment
—Advancing in the job

Demonstrating a good work ethic to your children goes a long way toward their own development of a work ethic. Learning to do chores, following instructions, and sticking with a task are important skills in obtaining and maintaining a job. If possible, getting a job in the teen years is a good start in learning how to work with a boss and coworkers and following the work ethic that parents have instilled in the teen.

11. Educational Skills

—Setting and reaching goals
—Developing study skills
—Having self-discipline
—Surviving and thriving in the university or technical school environment

If children do well with academics and proceed in school to higher education, it will help in getting a good job in the future and being able to support the family. Encouragement from parents to complete tasks, get good grades, and do their best will help to put the children ahead. When it is time to leave, a good foundation will have been laid for lifelong learning, which makes life much more interesting.

It is not always necessary for children to continue into higher education; it depends on which type of job fits their skills and talents. It's important to help children discover what is best for them and what is realistic so that they don't acquire heavy debt by going to college when it might be unnecessary or unfulfilling. One helpful resource is "4 Steps for Helping Your Child Set Effective Goals" at https://biglifejournal.com/blogs/blog/goal-setting-for-kids.

12. Interpersonal Skills
—Resisting temptations
   * Maintaining appropriate interpersonal boundaries

In a normal growing-up experience, the child is exposed to many social areas and has the chance to make and keep friends. Normal development and attachment are an important part of the foundation that parents lay for children so that normal relationships and boundaries can be developed.

Making sure you know with whom your children are associating, especially during adolescence, can help prevent future difficulties. Active and alert parenting is always key and helps to prevent disasters.

13. Dating and Relationships with the Opposite Sex Development of appropriate understanding of proper dating behavior and safety

—Having proper moral understanding
—Having respect for the opposite sex

It is vital that proper sexual education be provided in the home in such a way that rules of etiquette and morality, according to the Bible, can be maintained. This is an ongoing project that starts early in the life of the child. (See chapter 9, "Sexuality Education in the Home," and chapter 5, "Preparing for Marriage.")

14. Problem-Solving Skills

—Analyzing a problem
—Previewing the possible scenarios and solutions
—Formulating a plan
—Checking results

Issues often come up in normal conversation that indicate that a problem needs to be solved. Assist children in coming up with a solution by analyzing and previewing so that the problem is their own, and they can come up with what needs to be done, with the parent as the facilitator. The education systems in many countries do not assist children in learning how to solve problems but only how to memorize facts. Problem-solving falls largely to parents to pass this along.

Reading through the list above and discussing it is a good start; then you can see what is needed for a healthy launch.

It is important that children leave with a good relationship with both parents, even in a divorce situation. If children have anger toward one or both parents, they are likely to keep that anger throughout life, making it difficult to adjust to a job or marriage and family life. Forgiveness is an important concept if they want to be successful.

PART TWO

DEALING WITH
THE HARD STUFF

Facing the Challenges of Life

Introduction

We are called to minister to our families in all stages. This includes growing older (with all those challenges), facing illness, facing sin and betrayal, divorce, facing death, and many other challenges. We live in an imperfect, fallen world. Things go wrong. The body does not last forever. We were given a general guideline in the Noahic covenant that we would live to seventy years or, if particularly strong, to eighty. This is an average in healthy countries where people can get proper medical care. Many grow much older; many do not make it to seventy. Despite medical advances, however, we have not raised the lifespan much.

In part II, we will look at how to cope with the changes of life. For some reason, we seem to think that up until we are *really* sick, we simply will keep on going. Yesterday was no different from today. Tomorrow should be no different. We need to have a realistic view of the future—not being pessimistic but knowing that we are just passing through; this is not our final destination. We work on taking care of ourselves in the best way we can but with the knowledge that, eventually, something will take us and our family members out. We need to be secure in our beliefs and sure of our commitment to the marriage and to the extended family. Mental and spiritual preparation helps us to face the coming challenges.

Very often, when a spouse develops a serious chronic condition, the healthy spouse will decide "This is not for me" and will head out, leaving the ill spouse to fend for himself or herself. Rather, we need to look at such a situation as an opportunity to serve God in a special way, by caring for an ill spouse as much as we can.

Life often does not go the way we planned. God did not promise that our paths would be easy or that if we trusted in Him that all our problems would disappear, and we would be healthy and wealthy. He does promise, however, that He is with us through all our trials, even when we cause them ourselves.

Some of the typical stresses that occur with families are:

- A child becomes ill.
- A spouse becomes disabled.
- A parent becomes old and unable to manage.
- A family faces hard times (loss of job or home or too many bills).
- The father or mother leaves the home (divorce or separation).
- A family member (child, parent, grandparent, beloved aunt, or cousin) dies, whether prematurely or expected.
- A child becomes wayward and uncontrollable.
- Mental illness, dementia, or other challenges occur.

The world is corrupt and falling apart; *it is not the world God created* and said, "It is good"!

How does the church respond to the difficulties of life?

Pastors should review how the church assists its members with the difficulties they encounter. Ask yourself the following questions:

Is the church keeping track of her members so that if they don't show up, they might send someone to check on them?

Is the leadership and membership open to the hurting asking for help and prayer?

Are the families in the church strong enough to help each other when things happen? A strong family produces enough energy that they can be concerned with more than themselves, and they can be a good resource for the church.

Is there a ministry designed to help families deal with the hard stuff?

We will review some of the difficult issues that confront families with the hope that more churches will take on the challenge of helping their flocks to deal with the hard stuff, and families can be more aware of what to expect. This is not a comprehensive source of information but something to help families prepare for the hard things and to encourage the churches to minister more effectively to the hurting family. The bibliography in this book has a selection of helpful resources to continue the process, and there are many more sources available to help deal with the special situations that come up. The most important aspect is that we take care to have the resources to address situations as they occur.

11

Divorce

Unfortunately, many marriages do not make it. There are many reasons that couples are not able to stay the course. Sin of some sort summarizes the main reasons for reaching the point of divorce. Divorce is always difficult; children are always affected, even when a couple waits until late in life.

Laying a proper foundation for yourself, your home, and your family, based on God's Word, is very important and can provide the tools necessary to avoid this tragic outcome. God has provided some guidance on divorce:

> "I hate divorce," says the LORD God of Israel, "and I hate a man's covering himself with violence as well as with his garment," says the LORD Almighty. So, guard yourself in your spirit, and do not break faith. (Malachi 2:16)

> "It has been said, 'Anyone who divorces his wife must give her a certificate of divorce.' But I tell you that anyone who divorces his wife, except for marital unfaithfulness, causes her to become an adulteress, and anyone who marries the divorced woman commits adultery. (Matthew 5:31–32)

The guidance of the Bible on divorce is that it is permissible with adultery or if one is married to an unbeliever, and the unbeliever wants to leave. (See 1 Corinthians 7.)

In our corrupt and sinful world, divorce happens for a variety of reasons. Not all the reasons fall into the biblical framework, but we must remember that we all sin, we all fall short, and we may fail at marriage. There is forgiveness for this, whatever the reason might be.

Some of the more common reasons that marriages fail are among the following, taken from a variety of online resources

1. Financial problems. This seems to lead the causes in most surveys—a couple cannot discuss money; one is conservative with money, and the other likes to spend; no one is keeping track of the money. It might be too much money or too little money or enough money but the couple cannot communicate about its proper usage. (Having a program in the church or having those to whom the couple can be referred for help with finances before it becomes a problem might help to prevent this aspect.)

2. Communications problems. Too often, a couple does not take time to get to know each other by genuinely communicating on all levels prior to getting engaged. The couple must learn to be genuine and honest, to express real feelings, to learn how to resolve problems, and to talk about goals and dreams together. Too often, the relationship starts with the physical and never gets to the good communication skills. (See chapter 6, "The Ministry of Marriage.")

3. Family problems. There may be stress from in-laws, children, or stepchildren; differences in parenting approaches can result in an ongoing, progressively worsening conflict. This can be exacerbated by a child or extended family who has serious health or mental health issues. Finding ways for the couple to openly communicate and discuss the areas of disagreements can be very helpful.

4. Sex problems. Sex and intimacy are important parts of the marital relationship and the source of many marriage problems. Marriage must be consummated by the sexual act. Failure to consummate a marriage or problems with sexual frequency, quality, or infidelity are common reasons for a marriage to fail.

5. Outside-the-marriage relationships. Relationships with friends that were present prior to marriage may be a source of contention,

especially if they are opposite-sex relationships. Some friends may be intrusive and cause conflict. Sometimes a spouse might spend too much time with friends and not enough time at home with family. This may lead to wandering away from the marital commitment, so it can be a danger.

6. Addiction problems. (See chapter 18, "The Heartbreak of Addiction.") There are many ways an addiction can affect a marriage. Depending on the substance or behavior, the person's personality and mood may change to the point that he or she is not the same or does not act in a rational manner. The money spent on addiction can be extreme and put a great burden on the family budget. Sometimes, it reaches the point of domestic violence, which cannot be tolerated.

7. Abuse problems. Verbal, physical, or sexual abuse in a marital relationship can certainly be a cause of the failure of a marriage and should not be tolerated. The victim needs to remove herself or himself from the situation as soon as possible; too often, the delay is too long. (See chapter 12, "Domestic Violence.")

8. Incompatible personalities. The couple should discover if they are compatible prior to making the commitment of marriage, but it is often overlooked in the emotional and physical excitement of the relationship. Some traits in one may gradually become intolerable to the other. There are ways to work it out if the couple gets started on it soon enough, but as with many issues, this one often is left to fester for too long, until the couple no longer can stand to be together. During premarital counseling, a personality assessment tool can be helpful in uncovering incompatibility. One such tool is the Taylor-Johnson Temperament Analysis.

9. Disillusionment. Having realistic expectations of a marriage can help to prevent disillusionment. When the tough issues of real life hit, there is not a foundation to depend on, as the expectations of the relationship may have been unrealistic. What is it that the couple expects from the relationship? This question should be asked early on.

10. Time problems. The couple needs some time alone and some time together. Finding a balance between work, other obligations,

and home life takes planning and effort. Many times, one of the couple travels for work, may be in the military, or could be a truck driver who has to be away for extended periods. This is very hard on a relationship and can result in failure of the marriage, if not properly managed.

If we can educate couples about the causes for a breakup and ways to prevent it, many marriages could be saved.

Divorce is very common, even in the Christian community. The church must have a response to deal with this serious problem. We must be careful not to reject those who are going through or have gone through divorce and help provide needed resources to help them get back on track.

The church should provide:

1. Divorce prevention or referral for counseling, if not provided in the church
2. Marriage and family training, classes, workshops, and special sermons
3. Divorce recovery classes, support groups, and referrals for help
4. Assistance and understanding for the children affected by the divorce, with referrals for counseling, if not done within the church

Divorce, like any failure/sin we encounter, can be forgiven, and life can go on. There are, however, many consequences and disruptions that can result in serious problems.

As a church, we must be able to accept those who are broken from failed or failing marriages. We must not reject them but provide help and acceptance, recognizing that we are all broken and have failed God in many ways. He is able to forgive and allow second chances, so we also must also offer this.

As a divorced family, if children are involved, there must be a common focus on doing the best for them. Divorce is very painful for children; the effects may last a lifetime. There must be a way to help them get through it, as well as working on the coparenting aspects. The worst outcome is when the children become pawns for the couple to express their rage toward each other. Forgiveness is necessary, even if reconciliation is not going to happen. The goal of interaction would be only to deal with the children and their needs. If the couple are both Christians, it is hoped that the court would not be needed once guidelines are established.

Sometimes, if the door of opportunity is left open, the couple may work on their own issues and be able to come back together. This has to be done with care and much preparation, involving a counselor, when possible, and setting realistic guidelines and expectations.

12

Domestic Violence

The Christian marriage is supposed to be different from those of the secular world, but we all bring into the relationship our pasts, our cultures, our strengths, and our weaknesses and vulnerabilities. In many cultures, women are degraded or discounted in some way, and men are put in the role of dictatorial control. In some cultures, this leads to an acceptable mistreatment of women. Some have grown up in violent families that model improper treatment of each other in the family.

Jesus always honored women and even appeared first to women after His Resurrection. Women are often the first to come to faith in Christ in pioneer mission church-planting work and later bring their families. Men are a bit resistant at times. Men are the leaders and are expected to be the leaders in their families and in the church, but this does not denigrate the role of women, which is so important. As leaders in the home, men are to love their wives as Jesus loved the church—not an easy task, for sure. The role of the church is to help redefine the role of the man to be more in line with Bible teachings.

In many cultures, the concept is that women are lesser humans. They are thought to be owned by the men and need to be brought under control with abuse. It is often a difficult but necessary change in a culture as Jesus comes to reside in the family and community.

While my wife and I were serving in Africa as missionaries, we lived in the bush with a rather primitive tribe. Some had never seen white people, and some had never seen cars. One day the second wife of a new Christian came running into our house to hide from her husband, who was beating her for some minor infraction. I was not at home, but my wife, Ellen, was present. Fortunately, our small children were outside playing.

The man caught his wife, grabbed her, and started beating her with a stick. Ellen intervened and took many blows before he stopped hitting her. Ellen was able to calm him and, while she was still bleeding from the blows, explained to him that, as Christians, we do not treat women that way. He was a bit shocked at what he had done to the missionary wife— that she took the blows for his wife—and he seemed to take the lesson to heart, and the abuse did stop at that point. It was a difficult way to convey the lesson!

> Love is patient, love is kind. It does not envy, it does not boast, it is not proud. It is not rude, it is not self-seeking, it is not easily angered, it keeps no record of wrongs. Love does not delight in evil but rejoices with the truth. It always protects, always trusts, always hopes, always perseveres. (1 Corinthians 13:4–7)

This is the type of love that we are to manifest, and we can, as we allow God's spirit to control our lives and our passions.

The cycle of abuse has been well studied. Lenore Walker, in her classic study of battered women, *The Battered Woman* (1979), describes the cycle as starting with *tension* that builds from conflicts and internalized anger. This proceeds to an *incident*, in which there is verbal, emotional, or physical abuse. Usually, it will start with demeaning, insulting words and later to the physical. There follows the *reconciliation* phase. The "I am so sorry; this will never happen again" phase. Then there is *calm* for a time, or the honeymoon phase. This cycle repeats itself and will gradually worsen if no one intervenes.

This is a fairly accurate description in the many families I dealt with over the years in several cultures. I have seen that the pattern even starts during dating. The most common abuser is the male, but it can also occur that females are primarily responsible. There is a sense of control or jealous ownership of the other. Certainly, we need to be one-woman men and one-man women, but cutting the other off from other relationships may be the start of problems. This often proceeds when there is no intervention to control, and isolation of the other after marriage reaches the point that the other feels quite smothered. Control may then become financial—always shopping together, controlling the finances, tracking the other when he or she goes out, not trusting the other to be on his or her own. Jealousy then increases, sometimes to a level of paranoia. Then comes the argument and the issue that leads to verbal abuse, progressing to physical abuse and even more control.

According to a local resource at a domestic violence shelter, women endure the abuse for a long time. They will try to leave an average of nine times before they finally leave for good.

The damage to the self starts with the control and the instilling of a sense that the person is not good enough and that the "punishment" is deserved because he or she is so bad. This often becomes the belief system so that the abuse is endured for a long time before the victim makes it out of the relationship. Changing this belief system takes a lot of work in counseling, but most will recover if they can stay out of the abusive cycle.

Many women enter the abusive situation with a controlling husband based on what has happened to them growing up. They may have been abused or demeaned by an abusive father figure, so this feels OK; it is how life is, so they endure and life then becomes worse, to the point of being intolerable.

During a break from medical school, I was hired as interim pastor for a small church for a few months. I had some Bible training and was up for the challenge. I strongly believed in the marriage covenant and that we should do everything possible to maintain the relationship. I soon was faced with a marriage counseling situation. The wife asked for help, as they were not getting along. As I explored the situation in more depth, it soon became obvious she was experiencing rather severe physical and mental abuse. I advised her to leave the situation forthwith. I asked for help from others in the congregation to house her temporarily. I advised her husband to get help. If he didn't start to work on himself or show any progress, she was to proceed to divorce, which ultimately is what happened. I felt my first efforts in marriage counseling were a sort of failure, but in reality, there are situations that cannot go on without major changes occurring.

In premarital counseling, there may be signs of a problem, such as that the dominant partner does not allow the other to speak, interrupts to clarify the answers, or shields him or her from the counselor/pastor. There is a sense that many things are unspoken; the dominated one is allowed only to say certain things. At that point, the couple needs to seek professional counseling to deal with the issues before proceeding in the relationship.

In exploring the couple's history, there also might be cultural or historic issues. They may have been raised in an environment of misogyny (i.e., a negative view of women), physical and/or sexual abuse, or domestic violence in the family of origin. It may be beneficial to help the couple to be aware of that to avoid that type of problem. There is a high probability of repeating the cycle if it's not interrupted.

It is paramount that the church be aware of the situation and the symptoms of an abusive or potentially abusive relationship. In the United States, there are many domestic violence resources in which both partners can get help to make the necessary changes. Discover the resources for mental health and counseling in your area so that you will know what you can do in these cases.

As with any sin, there is the opportunity for forgiveness and restoration. In many cases of abuse, it takes time. The biggest risk is in coming back together too soon—the promises do not mean anything; the apologies have already occurred many times prior to seeking help. Words are not enough. There has to be action. There has to be the desire to get help and the focus to complete it. Much like addictive behaviors, there must be accountability, in which either one of the couple can feel free to call someone for help, and others will check to make sure he or she is OK. Often, it is necessary for the couple to separate during the process, taking care not to rejoin too soon. Supervision of the process is best accomplished by a trained counselor who is familiar with trauma and domestic violence. (See chapter 19, "Sin and Restoration.")

God calls us to peace. If the situation is dangerous or becoming that way, intervention must occur. Sometimes, lives depend on it.

Where changes do not occur and there remains high risk for abuse, divorce and legal involvement, sadly, may be the only recourse.

If there is violence toward children, in many countries it is the obligation of pastors or counselors to report the abuse to proper authorities. Sometimes, it is necessary to have the children placed outside the home while the parents seek help for themselves.

There are cultural differences in the way we raise our children. Abuse occurs when children are not treated as fellow human beings. They are children of God as well. We are entrusted with their care and must treat them with respect and not abuse or overcontrol.

Reasons that children might be in a dangerous situation include:

- Parents are using drugs or alcohol.
- The child has serious behavior problems.
- The child is mentally ill or autistic, leading to behaviors that are very difficult to manage.
- Parents are divorced or divorcing, and children are not dealing with it well.
- Parents lack skills to properly deal with normal behaviors.
- In a single-parent home, the parent is working and overly tired. He or she does not have help and becomes frustrated
- There is passive parenting—no or very little structure in the home—leading to out-of-control children and overreaction by the parent(s).
- A parent has mental illness and is unable or does not have the energy to properly deal with the children or to make proper judgments.
- There is lack of support from the extended family to provide guidance and direction for parenting.

Parenting is a difficult job, and it is easy to become overwhelmed. Before that happens, it is important to seek help from the church leaders or counselors.

The church must recognize that these issues may occur in the congregation. It may be necessary to offer parenting classes or make referrals to an agency that provides classes after taking care that these classes do not contradict the church's foundational beliefs.

Sometimes there are older women in the congregation, who have been good parents, who can mentor these younger parents to help them with difficult situations. This can be a very important ministry that can save children from harm and preserve the family structure.

The church, as a whole, is a family, and we must be about the business of caring for each other.

See the bibliography for items that can be helpful for church leaders.

13

Golden Years?

You work hard all your life, and now come the wonderful retirement years. Well, not so fast. Calling them the *golden years* doesn't seem to fit well— maybe someone was being a bit ironic to say so. Some enjoy the time away from work and make good use of those years. They are golden for a bit, but it does not last. Others find that it is now a full-time job to keep up with a deteriorating body. New complaints crop up as the years go by and other medications are added to the regimen. Sometimes it is also a full-time job to keep track of appointments for medical issues and keep track of all the medications. Gradually, if we live long enough, we find we cannot get around as well. Soon, we approach the end; the years have passed by so fast.

I have proposed the following question to many of my older patients: "What are your plans after retirement?" They often get a puzzled look, as most of them have not thought much about it. Many plan for the retirement years—all the fun they will have, all the places they will go. It is as though they think they will attain heaven here on earth, just by retiring. It often does not happen that way.

We spend very little of our time on this planet in this life. The life after is very much longed for and is very long (i.e., eternity). A sermon illustration I saw some years ago aptly helped with understanding this. The preacher brought a long rope to the pulpit, with the rope trailing off behind a curtain. On the end that he held, he taped about three or four inches with colorful tape. He mentioned that this taped part was our life here; the rest of the rope, which goes on forever, is eternity. What should we be invested in?

How do we ourselves handle the "golden years"? How does our family handle them?

How does the church best minister to those who have become what we might call "seniors"? These folks are generally retired and sometimes are active but sometimes cannot be very active. As we grow older, there are many challenges. I often hear from my older patients that growing old is not for wimps. As I am now in that particular group, I tend to agree!

There are many things to consider in helping the elderly. Already we have seen that there are issues of illness, dementia, mental illness, or caregiving stress. There are also a number of issues that are simply from getting older.

Accumulated Losses. There may be loss of spouse, children, friends, or coworkers as time goes by. The person may be in a state of grief frequently as these losses gather. This can be a setup for depression. Also, grief tends to lower our immunity to certain illnesses, particularly viruses, so this may lead to contracting more illness. Understanding the process of grief and assisting with counseling, connection with others, support groups, and so forth can help the elderly to get through this.

Isolation. With the loss of a spouse, the survivor often wants to live in the home they shared for many years. There is the risk, however, of becoming quite isolated. The only contact with others, if family is not involved, is at the store and church once per week. As the isolation progresses, it becomes easy to ignore signs of acute or serious illness, onset of dementia, risk of falls, or serious injury. The isolation may lead to no one coming by for days, only to then find the person in a seriously deteriorated condition. I have seen this too many times. As a church, we need to keep track of the seniors, especially those who live alone. Someone could check on them by phone on a regular basis to make sure they are OK. Also, someone might help them to get involved in a small group or senior activities.

Accumulated Medical Conditions/Illnesses. One of the more frustrating things about getting older is that our bodies, no matter how well we have cared for them, start to wear out. We have more aches and pains and the onset of various illness. The role of the church and especially the family is to encourage seniors to get the medical help they need and to encourage and help them through the process. Sometimes, having a companion, if there is no family around, to attend appointments with them can make sure the proper treatments are started and maintained.

Unoccupied Time. Seniors may be healthy, with skills that were used for many years in their professions, but now, suddenly, they are idle with nothing to do. Unoccupied time is an enemy that may lead to the temptation to use alcohol or to become involved in behavioral addictions. Prior to retirement, they must think about how their time might be used and look into volunteer activities or church or parachurch organizations that might need a hand. There may be hobbies, crafts, or artistic pursuits, all of which can be encouraged by church leadership and family members. Finding ways to stimulate the mind and memory, such as puzzles and games, can be helpful as well.

Senior Ministry. This is a vital part of the church. Seniors often have good energy to help out and to provide advice and counsel. Many churches do this very well. It is, however, part of the structure that the church needs to fully minister to families.

Some of the areas that should considered are as follows:

- Senior registry, with profile of the senior, living situation, any special needs, special talents, family involvement
- Senior mentors (seniors who can assist other seniors) who can visit and encourage those living in isolation or with distant families or who have special needs
- Companions to accompany to appointments and help make sure that the medical needs are met
- Activities, outings, special meetings, Bible studies during times that are convenient and provide some connections
- Other programming with the intent of providing *connection* with others, needed to maintain our connection with God
- Teams that go to nursing facilities, elderly group homes, assisted living, to visit, provide communion, and maintain connection with members or provide special music or devotionals.
- Opportunities for the healthy, capable seniors to serve in some way

As a church, we must care for our entire congregation. We are a family, and we need each other!

As a family, we need to understand the needs of our elder members, provide the care that we can, and make sure that we fulfill the command from God to honor our father and mother (this does not end when we turn eighteen).

> Do not rebuke an older man harshly, but exhort him as if he were your father. Treat younger men as brothers, older women as mothers, and younger women as sisters, with absolute purity. (1 Timothy 5:1)

We are told in the Bible to treat our elders with respect. The church needs to teach that, and our families need to make that a priority, especially if the older members do not live close by, where we can teach by example. Families need to be encouraged to take time with aging parents, to engage them in family activities if they are near, or maintain regular contact if they are at a distance. If there are special needs, the church leaders must point them in the right direction by having a list of appropriate resources in the community.

14

Dealing with Dementia

As family members age, certain diseases become more common; one of the more difficult conditions to deal with is the onset of dementia. The most common form of dementia is Alzheimer's disease, although there are others as well, and each carries its own challenges and difficulties. Knowing about the common forms of dementia and what to expect can be helpful for the leadership of the church and for the families involved. As a church, we need to help the families involved in these difficult situations.

The *Oxford English Dictionary* defines *dementia* as "a chronic and persistent disorder of the mental processes caused by brain disease or injury and marked by memory disorders, personality changes, and impaired reasoning."

We will review the more common forms to provide understanding of what to expect. They are as follows:

- Alzheimer's and associated diseases
- Frontotemporal dementia
- Huntington's disease (not so common but a real challenge)
- Dementia with parkinsonism
- Dementia from stroke or head injury
- Multiple sclerosis

Alzheimer's Disease

Alzheimer's is the most common dementia. It can occur, though rarely, as early as in one's fifties or early sixties—this is a form of the disease shown to be hereditary and more common in those who have the genetic marker for it. In general, it starts when individuals are in their late sixties and becomes gradually more common as they continue to age, to the point that a full 40 percent of individuals in their nineties are likely to suffer from it. The following are the main symptoms:

- Insidious and progressive memory loss
- Progressive difficulty in naming objects
- Progressive difficulty with speaking and understanding speech
- Gradual loss of ability to carry out manual tasks; initially, tasks such as brushing teeth or dressing; later on, self-feeding
- Loss of decision-making capacity and judgment (erratic, impulsive spending; becoming a victim of scams; buying items for friends; responding to ads on TV or social media to give donations or buy something)

Making the Diagnosis

In order to make the diagnosis of Alzheimer's disease, the physician will do the following:

- Clinical history (doctor takes a history of symptoms)
- CAT scan and/or MRI scan of the brain to rule out other causes
- Laboratory studies to rule out reversible causes
- Physical exam
- Specific testing of memory and brain function, particularly the ability to copy simple drawings or make a clock face.

Course of Disease

The disease often will last ten to twenty years from onset of memory problems, with a gradual progression over time.

- Initially, notable memory problems, more noticed by others
- Getting lost in familiar places
- Forgetting names of familiar people
- Losing track of thought in nondemand speech (can answer questions but derail when telling a story or explaining something)
- Difficulty carrying out normal and familiar tasks
- Subsequent further loss of memory function, long term as well as recent and remote
- Progressive loss of ability to perform activities of daily living (bathing, oral care, etc.)
- Loss of judgment; impulsive behaviors
- Possible development of paranoia (suspiciousness) and/or delusions (fixed false beliefs)
- Emotional incontinence (laughing, crying without context, overreacting to good or bad news, excessive crying with a sad movie or commercial, for example)
- Loss of expressive and receptive language
- Loss of control of bladder and bowel
- Loss of ability to walk or control function of limbs
- Loss of resistance to infections, eventually leading to the end

Goals of Treatment

Maximize function and quality of life in the following ways:

- Avoid unnecessary medication.
- Treat coexisting medical problems.
- Use medication to help memory issues.
- Treat behavioral disturbances and psychological discomfort.
- Keep the patient physically, socially, and mentally active.

It is important to accept the illness and work with it. It will not go away. Encourage the family to get the professional help that their loved one needs and to ensure that he or she is on the proper medication to slow the progression of memory loss. Someday, medication might stop the progression, but for now, we take advantage of the help that is available. We want to help families enhance the quality of life for the one suffering from Alzheimer's and for them to take care of themselves as well.

Support the Caregiver

The caregiver of an Alzheimer's patient requires support, which can be provided in the following ways:

- Recognize the caregiver's concerns and encourage him or her to seek help.
- Encourage the use of day care and respite care, if available. Members of the church can help provide respite for the caregiver.
- Encourage involvement of multiple caregivers, when possible, such as other family members.
- Encourage the family to educate themselves on the illness and treatment.
- Support the caregiver's efforts.
- Monitor the health of the caregiver; encourage the caregiver to seek regular health care for himself or herself.

When it appears that the stress is too high, and caregiving in the home is no longer an option, there may be options for other living arrangements, such as nursing homes, assisted living, or other such placements. The family needs to be encouraged to make the decision for placement.

Help can be found through the Alzheimer's Association at https://www.alz.org and www.alzheimers.org.uk.

Aspects of Other Dementias of Concern

Other forms of dementia will progress in a similar manner to Alzheimer's disease. The caregiver role also is similar, and the engagement of the church is the same. Other dementias provide additional challenges that we need to understand so as to respond to the family's needs as much as possible. Most of the above measures would assist the families with regard to other dementias as well.

Frontotemporal Dementia

This is one of the more severe types of dementia. It may start as early as an individual's late forties. There are many types of frontotemporal dementia, but the main type consists of the following:

- It often starts with impulsive, poorly controlled behavior. There may be the start of sexual indiscretions, affairs, or pornography, which formerly was out of character for the individual. There may be excessive spending, poor decisions, or sudden onset of use of alcohol and drugs.
- There is soon onset of repetitive words and difficulty expressing oneself.
- The individual gets stuck on ideas or plans and is hard to dissuade.
- There may be delusions (fixed false beliefs) early on.
- There may be some interaction with law enforcement before it is realized that the individual has a significant loss of ability to function.

Frontotemporal dementia is the most common dementia for those under sixty years of age. Help can be found through the Alzheimer's Association at https://www.alz.org, as well as the Association for Frontotemporal Degeneration https://www.theaftd.org

Huntington's Disease

This is a genetic disorder; the offspring of someone who has the disease have a 50 percent chance of contracting the disorder. Symptoms of the Huntington's disease are as follows:

- It often starts with a dance-like movement disorder that will worsen over time. Movements of arms and legs and around the mouth, which affects speech and swallowing, is called *chorea*.
- There is some intellectual deterioration, but generally, individuals know what is going on around them. Orientation is maintained; they are able to name objects but may lose speech and language in the later stages.
- Individuals experience loss of executive function, which includes poor decision-making, impulsivity, lack of a filter when speaking, and stubbornness.
- There is often lack of emotional control and mood swings.
- There is loss of control of anger for many, leading to verbal (yelling and screaming) and physical rage (violence toward objects or people).
- Individuals may become fixated on certain idea or plans.
- dividuals have poor toleration to change.
- The disorder may start when individuals still are in the prime of life—in their forties or fifties or, rarely, even younger
- As the disease progresses, individuals almost certainly will need assisted living or a nursing home.

It is important to understand that individuals hear and understand what is going on around them, even if they are not able to express themselves.

There is high risk of choking, as they often do not swallow well and tend to eat too rapidly or fill their mouths too much.

There is high risk for falls with the chorea.

Caregivers can experience a great deal of stress when trying to help out and deal with the many changes that occur throughout the course of the disease. The course of the disease is around fifteen years from onset of tremor to death. The caregiver burden is often too much; there is usually need for placement in a care facility.

Help can be found through the Huntington Disease Society of America at http://hdsa.org.

Parkinson's Disease Dementia

Parkinson's disease is a fairly common brain disease that most often starts in the senior years but can begin in the forties or younger. The onset is usually with a one-sided rhythmic tremor, slowing of gait, and maybe speech or swallowing problems. Cognitive issues generally are associated with Parkinson's disease, but initially, these are often not a major concern. There can be personality changes, such as becoming more rigid and less flexible, less tolerant of changes, and so forth. The disease can be managed for many years at home with medication for the tremor and adapting the home to prevent falls, and help with bathing and self-care. Over the years, the tremor may worsen and may be more difficult to control; there likely will be worsening cognitive problems. There may be a need for more care in the home or placement in assisted living or a nursing facility, if care is not possible at home.

The onset of cognitive problems indicates there is an associated dementia. This can begin any time in the course of the illness and is likely to be progressive. Most commonly, the memory issues start around ten years from onset of the tremor but can occur at any time. Medications can help to stave off the memory problems for a bit, but the disease will progress.

Most Parkinson's patients have changes in cognition and memory, mostly with being able to multitask and keeping more than one thing in mind. Some judgment and decision-making problems also can occur, along with problems with stubbornness and inflexibility. This often leads to poor safety awareness, leading to falls, which can cause injuries.

If the typical parkinsonian tremors start, and, at around the same time, there are hallucinations (usually visual) and loss of memory and decision-making capacity, this may be signs of a similar disorder called *Lewy body dementia*, which has a much more rapidly progressive course.

The American Parkinson's Disease Association offers more information and help at http://www.apdaparkinson.org.

Stroke and Head Injury

Stroke and head injury share common issues but can be very different. A stroke—more properly, a cerebrovascular accident (CVA)—occurs when a blood clot blocks a particular vessel serving a particular area of the brain or when there is a bleed from a vessel serving a part of the brain. Depending on that part of the brain's purpose, deficits will develop. If you hit the motor area, there generally is paralysis or weakness of arms or leg. If you hit the speech and language area, there is difficulty in expressing yourself or understanding what others are saying, called *aphasia*.

A transient ischemic attack (TIA) is like a stroke but the deficits will go away within twenty-four hours. If the deficits stay, it was a stroke.

A stroke can be mild, affecting only a small area, and the patient could recover fully or partially. It also may be devastating, leading to total disability, with need for total care in the home or in a nursing facility, or it may cause sudden death.

After a confirmed stroke, the physician often prescribes medication to address the cause, such as irregular heart rhythm. If the stroke was caused by a blood clot, blood thinners will be started to prevent the blood from clotting and causing another stroke.

Post-stroke rehabilitation—physical, occupational, and speech therapies—may be necessary. The full recovery potential from a stroke or brain injury is not known for up to a few years from the event. Improvement may be slow or sometimes without much change. Rehab can be difficult. The patient needs to have strong support and encouragement.

After a stroke, there may be depression. This can be a result of the stroke and not just that individuals have had a serious change in their lives. Medication for depression is almost always necessary. If the spouse or caregiver notices the change in mood, it is imperative to get the proper treatment, as depression is one of the most potent blockers for progress in rehab from a stroke or brain injury.

Brain injury can be a one-time incident or something that occurs with repeated head trauma, such as those involved in boxing or other contact sports, such as American football, or several accidents over time in which there is a loss of consciousness. This is called chronic traumatic encephalopathy (CTE). It can lead to many problems that are similar to progressive dementia, but it begins much earlier in life. There can be memory loss, depression, mood swings, and/or violent, impulsive behavior. This can lead to serious issues in the family. Professionals who are familiar with CTE need to attend to the condition.

Brain injury can affect many parts of the brain, just as with stroke. If the injury is severe, there is a higher risk of dementia occurring in the later years.

It is important for individuals to work hard in rehabilitation, when that is available, as the brain can heal, and they can improve from the initial deficits. Generally, but not always, the recovery that the individual has attained by two years is what he or she can expect to be left with.

I did have one patient who lost his ability to understand numbers due to a motor vehicle accident. About five years after the accident, he called me to say that he was heading back to his accounting job, as he had regained his ability with numbers. That is rare but does give some hope.

Further help and information is available at the Brain Injury of Association of America (BIAA) website at https://www.biausa.org and at Stroke Survivors Can, https://strokesurvivorscan.org.

Multiple Sclerosis

This is a tragic disease that affects young adults through later middle age, but it sometimes affects children. It occurs mostly in temperate areas and is much less likely in the tropical zones.

Multiple sclerosis (MS) is an autoimmune disease, in which the body's immune system attacks the lining of the nerves, the myelin sheath, making the nerves respond slowly or not at all. It can affect many areas of the brain and spinal cord. It often starts quietly with a few symptoms that come and go. There may be double vision; numbness in a leg or arm; stroke-like symptoms, such as temporary paralysis, difficulty speaking, or weakness; or any number of mild neurologic symptoms that may seem inconsequential or could relate to other disorders, as well as the onset of MS. These are called clinically isolated syndromes. Over time, they may become more frequent, leading to a visit to a neurologist; specific imaging makes the diagnosis. The disease may be mild—just an annoyance, with minor symptoms that last many years. There may be off-and-on moderate symptoms over the individual's lifespan, from gradual impairment of overall function to serious disability.

It also can be quite devastating, starting out with severe symptoms, such as inability to walk or coordinate hands, cognitive impairment, or visual impairment. My patients often describe the cognitive problems as "Swiss cheese brain," in which there are some memories of recent events but some are just gone, sometimes the important ones. Impairment can be progressive or come with the first attack and stay there.

Fortunately, there are many medications that can hold the symptoms at bay so that one may be able to manage quite well for a time. Many, however, progress into needing quite a bit of help. Common residual symptoms are fatigue and episodic confusion that may not resolve with the medications. There are often related psychiatric symptoms, such as mood swings, depression, irritability, and psychosis, which can be addressed with psychiatric medications.

Caregivers can feel quite stressed from the variable symptoms of the disease. Some days are good, and some are very bad. It is important that the caregivers obtain as much information about the disease as they can and share this with those in the church who might be able to provide assistance, when needed. The church needs to direct the family to agencies that can provide help and to encourage the caregivers to take care of their own health, as caring for a patient with MS can be quite exhausting. (*My Story* in chapter 15, "Chronic Illness and Caregiving," describes how this disease affected my family and me.)

Additional help can be found through the National Multiple Sclerosis Society at www.nationalmssociety.org.

Summary

The information provided above is a brief overview of some of the challenges that families face when these neurological diseases happen. There are many other serious neurologic illnesses that are equally devastating but rarer. It is important for church leaders to recognize the seriousness of the diseases and how they might affect the family and caregivers so that proper support and encouragement can be provided. Likewise, it is important that family members arm themselves with as much information as possible and work with medical professionals to provide the best care for their loved one.

Many other diseases that may occur may be considered rare diseases. When an individual suffers from a particular rare disease, family members need to find out everything they can about the disease so that they can inform church leaders; then those leaders can understand what it may mean to them and what might be expected of them, especially how they can help when needed. Information can be found at NORD (National Organization for Rare Disorders) at http://rarediseases.org.

15

Chronic Illness and Caregiving

One of the more challenging aspects of living in this world is caring for a loved one who is ill. Most marriage vows mention "in sickness and in health." but when we actually face that aspect, it can be quite a challenge. Many conditions and diseases result in someone in the family adopting a caregiving role. Some of the caregiving may last for years; some may be a matter of months, as the loved one passes because of cancer or has a prolonged recovery (or not) from a major surgery. The church needs to understand and respond to the special needs of caregivers, which they can do in many helpful ways.

My Story

My story illustrates some of the challenges and blessings of caregiving and may provide some understanding of the challenges. Sometimes, God derails our plans for His own plans. We can choose to follow humbly and find the blessings therein, or we can choose to be angry and frustrated about the situation and never share in the blessings.

My first wife, Ellen, and I were married in 1976 and planned to spend our careers on the mission field. She was a Bible college graduate, trained as a teacher, as well as a missionary kid, having been born and raised in India. I was still in medical school, with the plan to become a medical missionary, but *my* plan was not necessarily God's plan. We managed to serve on the mission field a total of five years in India and Kenya and ultimately in Mexico, where we first started to notice some problems.

Ellen injured her back while swimming with some of the kids at the orphanage where we served. One of the boys was pulled violently by a strong wave. She worked hard to pull him back, but in the process, she nearly severed a nerve in her lower back. She required emergency surgery and did seem to recover at first, but she gradually worsened. We had to return to the States, not due to her health but my own—I had developed breathing problems in Mexico City, not an uncommon situation.

We tried to find help for her back pain and gradual loss of mobility but were not successful. She was sent to a pain specialist, who did help some. Then one day, suddenly, she lost her ability to walk and had to use a wheelchair from then on. She continued to teach full time, and her students helped her to get around. I then noticed she had significant problems with judgment and with spending money. I had to remove the credit cards and hide the checkbook. I later found out from our grandson in her kindergarten class that she was losing track of what she was doing, and the kids had to remind her of her next step.

One day, Ellen collapsed at school and became unresponsive. Emergency medical services took her to the hospital. Medical personnel were not sure if she had a stroke, as her blood pressure was quite high. She was placed in the ICU for observation but nothing was noted. She was sent home, but an MRI was ordered for later in the week.

I went with her to the MRI. The technician was a bit disturbed by the pictures and asked me if she had neurologic issues. I saw the lesions in her brain. I called a neurologist friend to come to the MRI room to look at the films, which were not good news at all. There were some very large lesions, and it appeared that she was suffering from multiple sclerosis.

She found she could no longer teach. She was able to manage at home OK, using an electric mobility cart to get around. During the next year, she began to lose her vision and became much more forgetful. We hired a forty-hour-per-week caregiver to help out during the day. She gradually needed help with almost everything. I provided all her care on weekends and evenings, which at first was not very difficult.

She still had short times when no one was at home, and she was able to get the things she needed. One day, however, I arrived a bit late to find her unconscious on the floor. When she got to the hospital, we found that now she had diabetes and a blood infection from her urinary tract and gall bladder. She was in the ICU for three weeks and had two surgeries and then was able to discharge to a nursing home. We tried to get her home after a month, but that did not work so she stayed another month.

We moved into an apartment in town, close to the hospital, as she kept getting dehydrated and going into kidney failure. We needed more help at that point. As I mentioned, I was the weekend and night caregiver, but that eventually became too much. I had been able to get away to teach my Sunday school class every week but had not been able to attend church for about a year.

Gradually, her friends from church started finding ways to help. One lady took Thursday nights so I could stay in a hotel and get some rest. Another came on Saturday at noon, bringing lunch and staying the afternoon with her, reading to her and talking, which was a big help. I was able to get to my job on weekends—I worked every other weekend at the hospital at that time, as well as full time during the week. When a couple from church, who attended Saturday services, found out that I had not been able to get to church, they decided to come on Sundays so I could get to church and to work afterward on the weekends when I was on duty. This was a great sacrifice for everyone and very much appreciated.

I was able to manage fairly well with that help in place, but prior to that, I had one weekend that was very bad. When I arrived home on Friday night after work, I saw that she was not doing well. She was restless and uncomfortable.

She was up all night that night, rather confused and psychotic, and then was awake much of the day on Saturday. She needed a good deal of help but was not very happy with me. She then was up much of Saturday night. On Sunday morning, I called a nurse at the hospital, who I knew well and who had taken care of her previously, and told him that I was not doing well. I had not slept for two days, was emotionally distraught, and was basically in tears at that point. I was totally worn out—burned out, really.

He was able to leave his unit with a wheelchair and came to the apartment. He transferred her to the wheelchair and transported her to the hospital. He was then able to talk to the internist on duty there, who admitted her for dehydration. At that point, she always had something that needed a bit more attention so she stayed in the hospital for three days.

I slept for about eighteen hours and then was able to get back to work the next day. Caregivers can become completely burned out. I was in good health, so I was able to endure it well, but others have literally worked themselves to death—I have seen this firsthand in my geriatric practice.

If I had not received the help from her friends at church, I would not have been able to maintain myself and her. Their help was vital, and they considered it a ministry to her.

In-home care lasted for several years. During her last year at home, she required almost total care—she did not do well in the bathroom and could not walk at all. Transfers from bed to commode or wheelchair became more and more difficult. I fell twice while transferring her to a bedside commode. The second time, it was a struggle to get out from under her and to get her up—it took more than an hour. After that, she was agreeable to going to a nursing home.

She was transferred to a nursing home where I was medical director. The friends continued to provide help. One of her friends took it upon herself to bring Communion every week and provide some devotion time. We were able to get online church services, which she enjoyed. Of note, there was never a visit from pastoral staff during her seven years of not being able to attend services. She might have been on the prayer list a few times, but that was all from the church staff. God's people, however, were of great help.

We continued with a sort of normal life. I would work all day on Mondays at the home where she resided and spend every evening there, as well as weekends. I had Saturday evenings and Sunday evenings for myself. I was able to get back to church and be involved somewhat.

One morning, she called me on her cell phone before I had left the house. This was a surprise, as she had not been able to figure out how to use the phone since I got it for her. She could answer it but never called from it. She wanted some shampoo and lotion—that was all. I was very encouraged as she had not talked much over the past several weeks, even when I was with her.

I was looking forward to the day. I was to work at the nursing home all day. She was awake when I arrived. I spent some time in the morning, talking with her, but she was not as talkative as I had hoped. I helped feed her at lunch. All seemed to be normal. I helped her get back to bed after lunch. When I checked on her a few hours later, I found her in a seizure episode unlike anything she'd had before. She was unresponsive and never regained consciousness.

During the following week, I summoned her sisters and brothers to come, as it did not appear that she would survive. She was comatose for about a week, and on my visit the next Sunday, she did not appear to be breathing well. She was actively dying. I had asked God that I not be there when she went, so He arranged for my daughter and son to be there. They were on their way out to dinner but suddenly knew they had to get back to the nursing home to check on their mother. As they arrived, she took her last breath and was gone. They were able to be at her side, which was something precious to them. I came in quickly from home and was with them and the rest of the family as they gathered.

During the funeral and subsequent difficult weeks, I only had my family and her close friends to lean on. No one from church offered any help.

The weeks and even months after the loss of someone close are very difficult. This is a time when the church needs to be aware of the special needs of the grieving.

During the time I was in the caregiving role, I rather resented it at first. I was to be a missionary, a full-time servant of God, preaching and teaching in various countries. I soon realized that I was assigned by God to the *caregiving* role. I needed to do my very best in that role to please Him and to care for the one I loved so much.

Our assignments from God can be challenging and difficult, as in the role of caregiving. The blessings of obedience to Him are the same, whether He assigns us to preach to thousands or to care for the one we have at home.

The church has a cradle-to-grave responsibility to offer necessary help for families as they go through the difficult moments. Many leave the church after a difficult loss because they did not feel supported and loved through the ordeal. My church friends and coworkers helped me get through it, but I would have appreciated some concern from the church staff or elders.

Care for the Caregiver

The first priority, as a family, is to make sure our loved ones have what they need and to provide care for the one who is ill. If we are not able to provide that help, we should assist with getting the proper care through agencies or from church family.

What can the church do to help those who are involved in helping an ill or handicapped family member? Consider the following:

1. Know your community resources so you can make referrals to agencies that might be helpful.
2. Find a way to track members who are caregiving or in a difficult situation so that the church family can help, if needed.
3. Check on the family periodically to see if anything is needed.
4. Check on the caregiver's health (e.g., does he or she need to be encouraged to get some rest, a respite, or a medical checkup?).
5. Check on the caregiver's spiritual life (e.g., is he or she upset about caregiving or angry with God? Is he or she unable to attend services?).
6. Check for signs of burnout. The caregiver may appear mentally and physically exhausted and may not address his or her own medical issues. He or she may not be eating right or sleeping well and may not have personal time to relax and restore energy. The caregiver may need to be referred to a medical provider for help.

The church can develop a list of those in need and make notes of what they need and how to serve them. Volunteers can be recruited and assigned to visit and check on these families. The volunteers would have access to the information about those in need and how they could help. Many seniors are capable of helping out in this type of ministry.

As a church, we must ask ourselves:

1. Are we aware of what is going on in our congregation?
2. Are we able to encourage members to be actively involved in ministry to others?

3. Are we able to encourage those in caregiving roles to see that their work is indeed serving God in a special way?

The Bible instructs us to share our burdens, which is very necessary.

> Carry each other's burdens, and in this way, you will fulfill
> the law of Christ.
> —Galatians 6:2

16

Grief and Loss

One of the very important roles of the pastor and leaders in the church is to assist with grief and loss in the congregation. Performing funerals is only a small aspect of this important role. Understanding and dealing with the many types of losses can help those in the church to deal with loss effectively and not be diverted from their faith. So often, a great loss or setback will send those not fully grounded in the faith away from the church, angry with God.

We arrived in West Pokot, Kenya, in 1982 to work in a small mission compound, consisting of some houses, a clinic that was just being built, and a church. The area had been devastated by frequent battles with enemy tribes, and a recent drought resulted in no crops. Starvation and disease were rampant, including a dysentery epidemic. During our first week in the area, many babies and children died—and mothers wailed—and some adults also passed from the epidemic. After the main crisis passed, in which we lost maybe forty babies and children to dysentery—although many more were saved—we discovered that the tribe had lost many of their rituals. There was no funeral or burial ritual, which had been lost due to the frequent enemy attacks. Death was so common that bodies were along the roads.

We took time to start a burial ritual for the community to help with the grieving process. This resulted in a significant reduction in anxiety and depression, as well as people coming to the clinic with obscure symptoms for which nothing would be found. This was most likely *psychosomatic*—symptoms that developed because of psychological pain.

We need a way to structure our grief. It is very painful to lose a loved one—a friend, a spouse, a child, a parent. American Christian culture has a number of rituals. We may have a service in church. This may include a viewing of the deceased in a casket on the night prior to the funeral and then a service that consists of scripture, prayer, a remembrance of the deceased, and even time for attendees to speak of memories of the departed one. There is often a short message that reminds us of the promise of heaven. We then often have a trip to the burial grounds and have a short service as the body is placed in the ground. Some are cremated so there is a different type of service for them.

Other cultures may have a wake—a gathering on the night prior to the funeral to grieve together. A wake can be very emotional and passionate, but the process seems to help in dealing with the loss.

There may be special rituals at the graveside, such as placing cherished items with the loved one or placing some dirt on the casket after it is placed in the site.

These are some of the ways we structure our grief to make the process a bit healthier, allowing *closure* to the process. During the recent COVID-19 pandemic (2020–22), there was a time when funerals or gatherings of any type were not allowed. This resulted in many not being able to grieve the loss and caused some to have psychological problems as a result. The process of grieving is very important.

In grieving, we also deal with other changes in our lives. It is important to realize that other losses may result in intense emotions and a period of sadness, tears, and withdrawal, much the same as when someone important passes away. Consider feelings that might result from the following life events:

- Loss of job or career
- Retirement, with loss of purpose and identity
- Loss of marriage to divorce
- Loss of custody of children in a divorce situation
- Loss of a beloved pet, especially for those living alone, with the pet as their only companion

- Loss of mobility, now having to use a walker or wheelchair
- Loss of cognitive ability due to an injury, stroke, or dementia
- Loss of a limb due to accident or illness
- Loss of future due to a diagnosis of a serious illness or condition

When we experience a loss, we expect grief, a little bit or a great deal, depending on the *meaning* of the loss to us. If we see that someone has had an important loss in his or her life, we can better respond with love and understanding. For example, if someone relates to us that she lost her pet, we may wonder why she is having such a struggle. This loss, however, may have special meaning to her, and we must seek to understand, rather than to judge.

As we seek to help someone with a significant loss, we must be willing to sit and listen. We should not play it down but accept what the person's feelings about the loss so that he or she can proceed with the process of healing. With many losses, we cannot just put them behind us and go on. Some are so serious that we are deeply affected for the rest of our lives.

In the event of a serious loss, such as the death of a loved one, people may be very supportive at the time of the loss and offer support during the funeral. After the funeral, however, everyone leaves and goes on their way, and they often don't attend to or check on the ones most affected by the loss. Their pain is most acute in the weeks that follow. It's important to have a supportive pastor or church staff to check on them, a support group, or encouraging family members to provide support while the acute phase is going on.

Some cannot seem to get over the grief and will need to have counseling to help talk through and deal with the loss. Church staff need to know where to get this kind of help, if available, or provide counseling, especially on the spiritual side.

Many become angry with God that He would allow such a thing to happen to them. Working through this is very important so that we can stay connected with God and the church. It is OK to be angry, to express it, and to deal with the emotions and then come to the point of knowing that God is with us through even the most difficult losses. He stays with us through those who surround us to help us.

The process of grief is dependent on many factors. The type of loss as well as its meaning to the individual makes a difference. The experience of grief depends on the resilience of the individual, underlying conditions, such as a mental or physical illness, and prior experiences of grief and loss. Some may recover quickly—don't judge harshly, thinking maybe they did not care. Some take a long time, and we need to be understanding of that as well; we should not push them to put it behind them and go on with life. When intense grief goes on more than a few weeks, professional intervention may be needed.

The shortest verse in the Bible is John 11:35—"Jesus wept." This verse says so much on how we should respond to the heartache of others. Jesus deeply felt grief Himself but also for the others in the household.

> God's Love and Ours
> Dear friends, let us love one another, for love comes from God. Everyone who loves has been born of God and knows God. (1 John 4:7)

17

Understanding Mental Illness

⌒✍⌒

Approaches to Mental Illness

We need to be educated about mental illness, but that is often neglected or associated with shame. Mental illness is just another part of the corrupt body not doing well and needing the help of professionals to manage it. Many people in every congregation suffer from mental illness but there may be more who do not feel welcome.

The church response should be as follows:

1. Educate staff with the material found in this chapter and material found on trusted websites.
2. Get to know those in the congregation who are suffering chronic mental illness.
3. Find out what their comfort level is and what they need to feel a part of the church.
4. Consider small groups for support or Bible study, led by someone who understands mental illness.
5. Check on those members when they are not present. Phone or text them to make sure they are OK.

The family response should be as follows:

1. Learn about the illness to understand how it affects the family relationships.
2. Encourage those afflicted with mental health issues to get help.
3. Be accepting of the person. Understand that some behaviors are a product of the illness.
4. Find support from others who are dealing with similar issues, from social media, and from local support groups.

One of the more difficult tasks for many Christians is understanding the reality of mental illness. Some churches teach that mental illness is only spiritual and does not need anything but a spiritual approach. This has led to discomfort and a sense of rejection for those who suffer from chronic mental illness.

When symptoms of mental illness occur, often the first place Christians will go—and even some nonbelievers—is to the church. Pastors and church staff need to understand and accept the reality of mental illness. They must learn how to best help the families and those suffering and not reject them or spiritualize the issue.

To better understand how to help those who suffer from mental illness, we need to provide some answers to common questions.

Recently, the trend has been to call this area of medicine *behavioral health*, to which I do not subscribe, as mental health disorders affect the brain and mind and so are considered mental disorders, not something you have because you behave badly.

We can easily accept that one can get diabetes, hypertension, cancer, or a host of other diseases, as we know the body is corrupt from the fall and is subject to all kinds of problems. We all have a sinful nature and a body that only lasts for a season on this earth. For some reason, however, we are not so easily disposed as to accept that the brain is also corrupt and has a host of disorders and diseases that can happen to it as well.

Is it for real? Most mental health problems are caused by a problem in the brain. Some of the changes in the brain can be seen on special scans, such as PET or MRI, especially what is called the fMRI, or looking at the brain as it is functioning. We can see that in depression, for example, parts of the brain are not working right, giving rise to the symptoms presented, such as apathy (not wanting to do anything), poor attention, sad mood, and poor motivation and drive. For those interested scholarly articles on this, along with images of the brain can be found on https://www.frontiersin.org and on the National Institute for Mental Health website found in the bibliography.

Don't they just need to snap out of it? That would be nice, but this is the cruelest approach and may lead to more serious illness or even suicide. When someone is suffering from, say, depression and is told, "You just need to pull yourself together and get moving," they can try as much as possible, but that will not change the problems in the brain that lead to the symptoms. Moreover, those may be the words that push someone over the edge.

Aren't the illnesses caused by the drugs the psychiatrists give them? The medications do cause some side effects, and if they are not properly administered, they can cause more problems than benefits. Medications that are properly adjusted, however, and a regimen that is designed to address the symptoms that are presented can save lives and get people back to a more normal life.

Isn't it just a spiritual problem? This certainly can be part of the problem, as we will see later, but often, it is not the sole problem. Spiritual issues can cause serious depressive or anxiety problems. As part of the process of healing, this needs to be addressed as well.

If we are just spiritual enough, won't it go away? I am sure that many who suffer a mental illness or even a physical illness have heard—and it hurts. They might be trying very hard to stay close to God, but the disorder is standing in the way. Being told by a pastor, church leader, or family member that they just need to be more faithful in their walk with Christ and then this will go away is often enough to drive them from the church to seek help in the secular world. Some are resistant to return to the church.

What is mental illness? OK, then, what is it, really? Mental illness refers to a collection of brain disorders that affect the individual emotionally, as well as often affecting perception—how he or she interprets what is going on around them. The disorders might affect energy, attention, concentration, and mood regulation. There can be hallucinations, delusions, severe anxiety attacks, excessive worries, and poor appetite to point of danger to the person's health. There can be intrusive, unwanted thoughts, compulsions, inability to determine what is real and what is not, and a host of other symptoms that can affect one's life and stability, severely or just as a bother. Mental illness can be fatal as the disease may lead to suicide or avoiding needed medical care for other serious conditions.

To best understand any illness that plagues us as frail humans with corrupt bodies *and brains*, we need to look at the full aspect of the disorder and all the ways it affects us. I have a word to help us get our minds around it: *biopsychosociospiritual*.

All illness has a basis in *biological* factors. Whether you suffer from diabetes or schizophrenia, something has gone wrong in a part of the body that needs to be addressed.

All illness can affect you *psychologically*. It can change your perspective on life, reminding you that you are mortal, whether it's high blood pressure, cancer, or a mental illness. Your perception of yourself can change. Confidence goes away, future life might have to change, and you grieve the loss of your former healthy self. These and many other factors all contribute to your symptoms and recovery.

An illness can affect you *socially*. Now your social network can be stressed. Your family has to deal with the challenge of the illness, change of routines, and maybe change of diet. You may become socially isolated, lose your job and economic support, and have to go on public assistance to survive, as you may now be so impaired that you cannot work. Your marriage suffers, and your spouse has to adjust to a new role. There are many possible scenarios from minor adjustments to catastrophic changes.

And an illness often can affect your *spirituality*, bringing existential questions, such as, why me? What did I do to deserve this? Has God abandoned me? Your relationship with God, your church, and your devotional and worship life might change or at least be challenged, but you are in need of the support of the church—not condemnation, not criticism, but understanding and help.

To understand the cause and effect of mental illness, we need to consider all four factors. To effectively treat mental illness and most other chronic disease states, we must consider and address all four areas.

The goal in the treatment of any mental disorder is recovery to the best possible quality of life. For some, it may mean getting back to a fairly normal life, with some minor adjustments. For others, it may be a lifelong struggle; recovery may be to the point of maintaining the best possible level of function.

We will review some of the more commonly presented mental disorders and discuss the best approaches and how these individuals are treated in the mental health system. First, we need to define the players and roles in the treatment process. You need to know on whom you can depend in the community for each level of treatment needed. There may be some Christian providers, but unfortunately, we are a bit rare in most communities.

Psychiatrists are medical doctors with either MD or DO (doctor of osteopathy) degrees in the United States. Other countries have a different set of initials, such as MBBS (bachelor of medicine, bachelor of surgery), which is equal to an MD or DO degree. The MD and DO have very little difference in their training. Once they have completed medical school, they will do postgraduate training in psychiatry and perhaps more training in other subspecialties, such as forensic (legal work), child and adolescent (a two-year fellowship), neuropsychiatry (treating illnesses that fall between neurology and psychiatry), addiction, and other areas. These are the most specialized to treat the various aspects of mental disorders.

Psychiatric nurse practitioners are nurses with an advanced degree that allows them to diagnose and treat mental disorders. Their background is less specialized than that of psychiatrists, but they are able to prescribe and manage many of the disorders. Often, they work alongside psychiatrists in private and public clinics. In the United States, there are also those called *physician assistants*; they specialize in mental health and are able to diagnose and treat many of the disorders. They work under the supervision of a physician.

Psychologists have a PhD or PsyD in psychology. They are able to diagnose mental disorders, provide talk therapy (psychotherapy or counseling), and do specialized testing. Some will have training to prescribe, in a limited fashion, medications for the disorders but most cannot prescribe medication. Those who do prescribe will have had additional training to do so, somewhat similar to the nurse practitioners. In other countries, the psychologist may have what would be equivalent to a master's degree, having studied the field for five or six years after high school to become licensed as a psychologist. They are able to do diagnostic testing and counseling.

Social workers usually have a master of social work (MSW) degree and master's level training in some forms of therapy. They can assist with formulating treatment plans for complex patients and with finding services. Many are employed in the hospital inpatient services; some in the community provide psychotherapy or counseling.

Counselors are providers who have a master's level of education in psychological counseling. They provide various forms of counseling to assist with attaining and maintaining stability for the mentally ill. Some patients mostly have psychosocial problems and may only need the counseling aspect to get back on track. Many need to have medical approaches as well as counseling, which has been shown to provide much more long-term stability for those suffering a chronic mental disorder.

In the United States, most states have a mental health system to assist with the more severe chronic mentally ill. If one is severely ill, demonstrates a danger to self or others, or is considered gravely disabled (unable to care for oneself; lacks judgment to keep safe or provide basic needs), there is the provision that the individual can be hospitalized against this or her will and be provided medications to stabilize. Some states use state hospital facilities, when available, to provide the longer-term treatment.

Some severe chronically mentally ill individuals not be able to care for themselves independently and will have to live to in assisted living facilities (ALF) or sometimes a nursing home (skilled nursing facilities). In some countries, the facilities might be referred to as asylums for the elderly, disabled, and mentally ill. Some countries have no provision for this as yet or may have long-term psychiatric hospitals with few options for treatment.

Meeting the spiritual needs of this population is very important and often overlooked.

The definitions of the forms of mental illnesses and more information regarding them can be found on the National Institute of Mental Health (NIMH) website and in the *Diagnostic and Statistical Manual of Mental Disorders* (DSM-V), found in the bibliography.

Now let's take a look at the more common mental illnesses and approaches that are needed:

- Mood disorders
- Anxiety disorders

- Psychotic disorders
- Trauma disorders

This is not meant to be an extensive review or to cover all the possible illnesses that are seen in a psychiatric practice.

Mood Disorders

There are several kinds of mood disorders and many symptoms related to them. They generally fall into the categories of major depression and bipolar disorder. The main problem is that the emotions or feelings do not correspond to the circumstances and may be expressed in an excessive manner.

Depression

Depression itself can occur in many situations and can have many causes; it's not always a biological mental illness. It can be the result of many illnesses, some medications, or circumstances in life. There can be a host of spiritual causes as well. When someone is evaluated for depression, we look at all the circumstances prior to determining if this is a biological illness or psychosocial. Sometimes, counseling and spiritual approaches are all that is necessary, but if there are major symptoms, as noted below, the pastor or counselor needs to be ready to refer to a provider who can address the medical issues. When the symptoms have crossed into a disorder, the symptoms are persistent, last longer than two weeks, and do not respond to counseling or change of circumstance in life, then it has likely become major depression.

Major Depression

This is a fairly common disorder. It may occur on its own without any circumstances seeming to provoke the symptoms. Onset may be slow and insidious, not evident to individuals themselves sometimes but noticeable to those around them.

Common symptoms include:

> Sad mood
> Low energy
> Irritability
> Loss of appetite or sometimes increase in appetite
> Increased or decreased sleep
> Fatigue; loss of energy
> Discouragement; negative thoughts

Less common symptoms include:

> Suicidal thoughts or behavior
> Hallucinations, usually auditory
> Delusions, usually regarding self-annihilation (fearing oneself is already dead or believing one is rotting on the inside, for example)
> Paranoia (misinterpreting what is going on around oneself, to the point that one believes he or she is the object of persecution or manipulation)

Depression Occurrence

Over 20 percent of individuals, at some time in their lives, will suffer at least one episode of major depression.

The elderly are particularly vulnerable, due to accumulated losses and physiologic changes that might provoke the symptoms.

Depression is often underrecognized in the elderly, particularly those in long-term care.

Depression Causes

Major depression may occur spontaneously or may be provoked by stress, such as an unexpected loss or a physical illness.

Those with a family history of depression, other mood disorders, or alcoholism are much more likely to suffer an episode of depression.

Diagnosis

A thorough history laboratory and physical examination must be done to rule out other physical or psychiatric causes of depression and to make sure of the diagnosis.

It is not uncommon for bipolar disorder (discussed later) to be missed without a good history and examination.

Psychiatric Illnesses That Cause Depression

Schizophrenia is often associated with a depressed mood, especially at the time of the first break; that is, the time of the onset of the first severe symptoms. It is important to address the depression as well as the primary disorder.

Bipolar disorder may cause depressive mood swings. Often, patients will forget to mention that they also have very high, or manic, swings, so we think it is just depression.

Anxiety disorders may progress into major depression during the course of the illness.

Physical Illnesses That Cause Depression

Dementia of all types, but more often in parkinsonian dementia, almost always can easily be missed and can result in worsening of cognition. With treatment of the depression, quality of life and cognition can improve, at least temporarily.

Multiple sclerosis, especially later stages, may also show mood swings similar to bipolar disorder or depression, which is often from the effect of the MS on the brain.

Certain cancers can start with an episode of depression.

Chronic pain has a strong effect on moods. As the pain persists, there is more discouragement and difficulty with functioning. Treatment of the depression can help individuals to deal better with the pain. Treatment can also be psychological with use of counseling to deal with the pain.

Brain tumors in certain areas of the brain can result in profound depression as a symptom. Even some infections, particularly viral, can result in temporary depression. For these reasons, it is very important to undergo a medical and psychiatric evaluation to provide the best approaches for the depression.

Diabetes mellitus, especially when there are rapid changes in the blood-sugar levels, can result in depressive symptoms. These often are relieved with good glucose control.

Some strokes may be complicated by depression.

Thus, it is very important that the individual presenting with symptoms of depression be evaluated to rule out other causes.

Biochemical Causes of Depression

The brain functions by wires that are connected by synapses, or spaces, along the wires. To transmit the current through those wires (axons), there is need for messenger agents that work in the space, or synapse. These are called neurotransmitters. Depression involves at least three major neurotransmitters: serotonin, norepinephrine, and dopamine. These mostly work in the front part of the brain.

Depression occurs when one or more of these are deficient or relatively deficient. The receptors that connect to these chemicals might malfunction as well. When these are deficient, the flow of current from one part of the brain to another (circuits) does not occur efficiently. This likely is a cause for the depressive symptoms. In part, the problem is likely that the neurotransmitters are not sufficient; also, the circuits might not be working well. Treatment is designed to increase the availability of the deficient neurotransmitters and to make the circuits work more efficiently.

Brain Pathology in Depression

The main area involved in major depression is a small area just to the left of the middle frontal area of the brain. It's part of the cingulate gyrus as well as the hippocampus, just inside the temporal lobe. Both suffer damage with depression.

On the positive side, both show cell growth and repair when depression is treated.

Treatment of Depression

- Counseling can be helpful but often will not result in resolution on its own. Certain forms psychotherapy, such as cognitive therapy, have been shown to improve brain function in the deficient areas.
- Some natural remedies can help: hypericum or Saint John's wort, omega-3 fatty acids, and valerian root. These are generally not effective alone but can be helpful.
- Medications are most often needed to improve the function of the brain and allow for some healing of the brain in the deficient areas.
- Over 70 percent of individuals treated with the first agent will obtain relief, but only 30–40 percent will have complete remission of symptoms.
- There is greater than a 30 percent chance that after one episode of depression, there will be a second one.
- After a second episode, there is greater than a 90 percent chance of a third episode.
- As standard practice, if there is a second episode, we recommend ongoing treatment to maintain stability. Most often, this will prevent further episodes, decrease the severity, or decrease frequency of further episodes.
- Most of those treated, especially with counseling and medication, do find relief, but there are those whose depression does not find relief, even with many different medications.
- When medications are not effective, ECT, or electroconvulsive therapy, is available as an alternative. It likely works by enhancing the circuits in the brain by stimulating them with an electric current while the patient unconscious—a massive release of neurotransmitters. TMS, or transcranial magnetic stimulation, is another way to enhance circuit function. A large magnet sends an impulse toward the part of the brain involved in depression, stimulating the circuits.

Bipolar Disorder

This is a cyclic mood disturbance resulting from dysfunction in the brain circuits that connect the cortex to the limbic lobe. The cortex is the outer layer of the brain. The limbic lobe is mainly on the underside of the brain and is largely responsible for emotional expression.

Onset is generally in young adults, but it is known to show up anytime in the life cycle.

Bipolar disorder comes in several varieties but mainly has to do with high energy/mood states, low energy/mood states, and shifting between those states (mood swings). The various classifications have to do with how high or low the moods are and how frequent. *Bipolar mixed* is very rapid changes. *Bipolar II* is little ups and big downs. *Bipolar I* can be manic (high) or depressed (low) or both, but to have the diagnosis, one must have the highs but not necessarily the lows. Some with bipolar never have the depressive swings.

Bipolar depression has the same symptoms as noted above for depression, but individuals may swing out of the depression quickly.

Mania is a state of high energy, minimal sleep, increased goal-directed behaviors, high impulsivity (not thinking before doing), erratic behaviors, and possibly grandiose ideas (thinking oneself to be powerful or special in some sense). There may be psychosis, which may include delusions, which are fixed false beliefs, usually having to do with believing oneself to have some special powers or grandiosity. There may be hallucinations, which are perceptual disturbances in which one may hear or see things that are not real.

Hypomania is a high-energy state that is generally productive and not generally destructive. Individuals may have racing thoughts and do not have any psychosis.

In children, the diagnosis of bipolar disorder is sometimes confused with attention deficit disorder, which has to be ruled out—or it can be a part of it.

As a pastor or church leader, you may see individuals presenting with highly religious behaviors, overactive talking, and being overly generous with money. They may or may not have unrealistic ideas or plans. Someone may show episodic suicidal behaviors and call for help frequently. This is a very serious illness, so if there are signs that lead you to think there is a serious mental health issue, make efforts to get the individual to a mental health provider to be diagnosed and properly treated.

Diagnosis

A psychiatrist will go about the diagnosis in much the same way as with depression (noted above), being careful to rule out any other diseases that might be causing the disturbance. Careful attention is paid to the character of the mood pattern. Information from family or friends is very important to clarify what is really going on.

Treatment

The approaches are mostly the use of mood stabilizers and sometimes antidepressants. The treatment is generally lifelong, as this is a chronic disorder.

If individuals present with these symptoms, it is important that you refer them to a provider in the community who can effectively treat them.

Prognosis

- With early onset in childhood or adolescence, the outcome may be good in most cases. Ongoing treatment is needed for most individuals, but in some cases, the symptoms resolve or are in remission for a few years.
- Most commonly, the onset is late teens to early twenties.
- Lifelong treatment generally is required.
- Most individuals remain stable on medication. Many new medications are effective for maintaining stability with few side effects.
- For some, probably greater than 30 percent, some cognitive problems occur in their late forties or early fifties that can make it difficult to maintain employment.

Anxiety Disorders

These disorders are very common and often easily treated. There is, however, a range of severity that is important to understand. Anxiety may be just a bother, or it can be severe and disabling, to the point the person cannot leave the home due to severe anxiety and panic. As we will see, a certain amount of anxiety is necessary to keep us safe.

It is important to be understanding of this disorder; do not blame it on the person's not being faithful or not trusting God. Some anxiety is related to that, and it is important to recognize it. We are advised in scripture:

> Humble yourselves, therefore, under God's mighty hand, that he may lift you up in due time. *Cast all your anxiety on him because he cares for you.* (1 Peter 5:6–7, italics added)

Why do we need anxiety? In order to sense danger and react appropriately, God designed a cool system in the brain. We take in information, and a part of our brain determines if it is important or dangerous. If it is dangerous, we are activated, ready to take on the danger or run away. Our hearts beat faster; we are alert and able to respond quickly, due to the increase in our anxiety levels. However, if we are on hyperalert and there is no danger, we have likely crossed the line into an anxiety attack. If this is an ongoing problem, we may even have an anxiety disorder.

When does it become a disorder? When the anxiety no longer serves a purpose to properly alert us to stressful situations, and it occurs on a frequent basis—to the point that we find it hard to manage, or it affects our lives and function—then we have crossed the line.

Many years ago, a pilot was referred to me for treatment of his depression. He related an interesting story about anxiety in his life. He was a cargo pilot. He and his family owned a fleet of older aircraft in good condition. After many years of flying and no incidents but a number of scary situations, he was confronted with a serious problem. He was about to land, fully loaded, in a small-town airport. All was going well until he engaged the landing gear.

You get three green indicator lights if all is in place; he had two. He pulled up the landing gear and tried again—once again, only two green lights. He requested a flyover to have visual on the landing gear. Sure enough, only two wheels were down. He decided he would have to belly land the plane. All was made ready for a crash landing.

He steadied the controls, lowered the flaps, and executed a perfect belly landing. The plane was foamed, and he was taken from the cockpit unharmed. When he was asked how he was, he indicated that he was just fine. He left the airport and went to a local motel.

In the middle of the night, he woke in a cold sweat. He realized suddenly that he had gone through what should have been a high anxiety-producing situation, but he had been cool and calm. He called his brother and partner and told him that he was no longer fit to fly.

His brother asked, "Why?"

He replied, "I have lost my anxiety. I am not a safe pilot." He explained to me that he would fly fearlessly in bad weather conditions and barely make it to land. There was no signal I in him that said, "This is too dangerous; turn back!"

Definition of Anxiety

Anxiety is a heightened sense of alert; being ready for a challenge, a danger, a sudden change. There is elevation of the heart rate, increased activity in the brain, and an increase in stress hormones and other activating chemicals in the brain. Anxiety produces a desire for "fight or flight." It is adaptive for stressful situations. The right amount of anxiety is needed; too much is not helpful and may even be paralyzing.

Generalized Anxiety Disorder

There is excessive anxiety and worry on more days than not, affecting life in some way. Worry cannot be easily controlled. Anxiety is associated with the following symptoms:

- Restlessness; being on edge
- Easily fatigued
- Poor concentration

- Mind going blank
- Irritability
- Muscle tension
- Sleep disturbance

Other Forms of Anxiety

Separation anxiety occurs when, for example, a child is fearful of leaving his parent and does not want to go to school due to fears.

Selective mutism is diagnosed when a child will only speak in certain situations with certain people.

Specific phobias include, for example, a fear of water, snakes, or certain places. This may come from prior trauma or from having had a panic attack when in a certain situation

Social anxiety is fear of being in social situations, around a large number of people, and having to speak to strangers or in front of people.

Panic disorder, with and without agoraphobia, is one of the more serious of the anxiety disorders. Without much happening around them, individuals suddenly develop severe anxiety—fast heartbeat, sweating, breathing very fast, having a sense that something bad is going to happen. They may become acutely suicidal and may run off to get away from the severe anxiety. Attacks may last minutes to hours; they may disrupt work or driving, may cause major social disruptions if not addressed. This can be confused with a number of medical disorders so is always important to make sure medical issues are ruled out.

Some individuals develop *agoraphobia*, which is a fear of going out. One day, for example, they are driving over a bridge when, out of the blue, a panic attack occurs. For them, the mind connects bridges with panic, so that the next time they approach a bridge, panic starts. So, they avoid bridges. Then the panic happens with other places and other situations, gradually closing down options to leave the house. Ultimately, leaving the house causes onset of panic, and they become housebound and fearful of going out. Agoraphobia literally means fear of the marketplace; it is a disorder in which you fear leaving your safe place. Rarely, some individuals are not even able to leave their own rooms.

Obsessive-Compulsive Disorder

In this anxiety-related disorder, the individual suffers recurrent, unwanted, repetitive intrusive thoughts (obsessions) and does recurrent, unwanted, repetitive actions to undo the obsessions (compulsions). There may be excessive handwashing with fear of infection or germs; checking and rechecking and doing things over and over until it is "just right"; rereading or rewriting over and over. When one is a bit obsessive-compulsive, one has a good sense of detail and is able to do things very carefully, which is a positive, but it crosses the line into a disorder when it becomes distressing and causes impairment in some area of life.

Related to the obsessive-compulsive disorder are other compulsive disorders that can seriously affect one's life and adjustment:

With a *hoarding disorder*, individuals cannot seem to discard what they consider important to them. They sometimes end up with a house full of stuff so that one can hardly find a place to sit or lie down.

With *compulsive gambling*, individuals cannot stop gambling, despite it costing them dearly, such as losing their home and family. This falls under addiction as well.

With *compulsive self-injury*, individuals (often teens) will find relief from stress by cutting on themselves, sometimes to the point of requiring suturing of the wounds.

There is also compulsive hairpulling (*trichotillomania*), skin picking (*dermatillomania*), and other "habits" that one cannot seem to control and that affect one's life.

Treatment Approaches

Biopsychosociospiritual

Many anxiety problems need to be evaluated by a physician and addressed with medication first—if symptoms are severe or life-threatening, that has to be the first approach, but we cannot stop there. People can learn to manage their anxiety through therapy and counseling, but they have to be calm enough to learn and respond. Less severe manifestations are adequately addressed with good psychotherapy approaches.

- A balanced approach is always best, addressing the biologic, psychological, and social aspects.
- Medications should be taken when needed and for the prescribed length of time.
- A good goal is to bring the patient to a point where medications are not necessary, but sometimes this is not possible.
- Addressing the spiritual underpinnings is always helpful and learning to put our full trust in God.

Biological Approaches

Many medications are helpful, especially some of the antidepressants, usually along with medication for the anxiety. The antidepressants will often calm the anxiety over the long term so that anxiety meds are not needed. It is not uncommon, however, for the medications to be continued for the long term.

Biopsychological Approaches

Learning to relieve tension throughout the day is very helpful and makes changes in the brain. Default mode is a type of brain function that is very helpful. We all do this but may not be aware of it. We stare out the window or at a blank wall but don't see anything; the mind just wanders. We can do it for a minute or two, and it is as effective as a nap in calming the brain and allowing us to proceed with the day.

The anxious person can learn to pay attention to his or her muscles. High anxiety leads to muscle tension, which leads to lactic acid in the muscles. High lactic acid can increase anxiety and lead to panic.

Exercise allows the lactic acid to leave the muscles, and it relaxes the mind. Walking several times per week can help. Anxiety is actually blown off in the form of carbon dioxide as the muscle tension releases. Massage therapy can effectively remove the lactic acid as well.

Aromatherapy, particularly the use of lavender or a 1:2 combination of lavender and peppermint can relieve headaches; numerous other combinations can be helpful.

Acupressure and acupuncture have been shown to have some benefit.

Psychological Approaches

Some psychological approaches for treating anxiety include the following:

- Providing information and training about anxiety to the individual.
- Helping make the unknown known and the unexpected expected; helping the individual to determine what is really important. ("I take responsibility for what I can control and don't take responsibility for what I cannot control.")
- Teaching the individual how not to go into excessive anxiety when faced with stress.
- Teaching individuals self-calming techniques; they take control over something that has complete control over them.

Cognitive therapy also is very effective. *The Feeling Good Handbook* by David D. Burns, MD, is an excellent resource to teach oneself how to control those responses and to tell oneself the truth of what is going on around him or her.

Sociologic Approaches

Sociologic approaches for treating anxiety include the following:

- Develop and maintain a good support system.
- Support the family structure.
- Work on the marital bond.
- Seek family therapy or couples therapy.
- Educate the support network to be helpful, understanding, and appropriate so they don't promote helplessness or withdrawal. They

should assist in reducing and managing stress in work and home environments.

Spiritual Approaches

The balanced approach includes the spiritual as well. Learning to trust more in God. The practice of praying as a first step when situations come to us and allowing God to guide us through the stress is very important.

> The LORD is my light and my salvation—
> whom shall I fear?
> The LORD is the stronghold of my life—
> of whom shall I be afraid? (Psalm 27:1)

Psychotic Disorders

Psychotic disorders are relatively rare. Bipolar disorder and severe major depression can result in psychotic symptoms, as can some other disorders. The most severe of the psychotic disorders is that of schizophrenia. The symptoms of psychosis are any of the following:

- Delusions: fixed false beliefs that defy logic, reason, or contradictory facts. (Sometimes, these may be religiously based.)
- Paranoia: being suspiciousness of others, fearing harm to self or others, deriving negative or personal messages from otherwise neutral interactions or input, misinterpreting the intent of others, finding meaning in otherwise unimportant input. These result in lack of trust. This can deeply affect a marriage, as there are accusations of all kinds that may not be true.
- Hallucinations: abnormal sensory experience unrelated to external stimuli.
- Visual: *complex*—sees human or animal figures with or without audio; *simple*—sees colors, shapes, amorphous objects.

- Auditory: *complex*—hears a voice or voices with understandable output, which can be commands or commentary; *simple*—hears just a noise that might be hard to define.
- Tactile: a sense that one is being touched hit, cut, etc.
- Gustatory: unstimulated sense of what is usually a foul taste.
- Olfactory: unstimulated odor, usually very disgusting.

Schizophrenia is a chronic, disabling psychotic illness. It causes the patient to suffer from delusions, hallucinations, and disordered thinking. There may be language disturbance. There is often a sense of being controlled by external forces. The disorder is chronic and often progressive. If onset is during childhood, the prognosis is less positive, and the child likely will need long-term assistance. It most commonly occurs during late adolescence to early twenties. Rarely does it occur after age thirty-five. There is waxing and waning over the years with some deterioration after each psychotic episode, which is a time in which the symptoms of psychosis become acutely worse, usually leading to hospital confinement. The more episodes of acute psychosis there are, the worse the overall cognitive and social function will be later in life.

Types of Schizophrenia

- Paranoid: predominantly paranoid or grandiose delusions; language is unimpaired, generally.
- Undifferentiated: might have paranoia, disturbance of language, mood instability, or catatonia (becomes immobile, unresponsive, or hyperactive but unresponsive).
- Disorganized: occurs rarely; profound language disturbance. Delusions are fragmented; severe hallucinations. Disorganized schizophrenia is hard to treat, and the patient often becomes demented.
- Schizoaffective: often categorized on its own. This disorder has prominent schizophrenic-type symptoms, with either mood swings, persistent depression, or persistent mania. It might look like bipolar disorder or depression, but the thought disorder (psychosis) persists and has symptoms like those of schizophrenia.

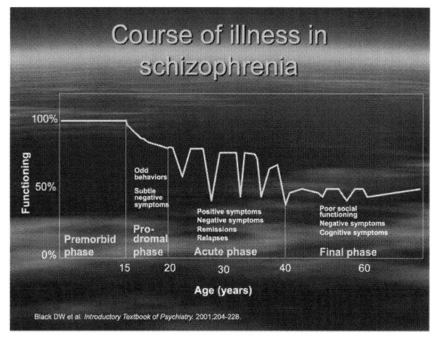

Schizophrenia is a slowly progressive disease.

Janet was only eleven years old when the voices started. They were just once in a while but rather disturbing. She would hear that she was ugly and fat and should not be alive. She would often think of how she might end her life, but she did not do anything about it until she was nearing her eighteenth birthday. At that time, the voices became very strong. She started to believe that her parents were evil. The commands to harm herself also became very strong. She finally confided in her mother that her thoughts were just not right and that she was not feeling good. She could not tell her about her voices and other symptoms. She did ask to see a doctor.

She was taken to her family doctor, a Christian, who listened carefully to the symptoms and assured Janet that she could get some help. She was sent to a psychiatrist who was able to fully evaluate her and get her on medications that stopped the voices and slowed down the impulses so she could be safe. The family was provided with information on schizophrenia and what they could expect.

The youth leader of Janet's church was told in confidence of her issues and was provided with information on the disorder so he could help. Janet had plans to attend college, but her symptoms made it hard to complete high school, even with the medication. She tried a few classes but the voices were too intense when she tried to concentrate. Her family was able to find assistance through some agencies to obtain ongoing treatment and part-time employment. Janet would require help throughout much of her life. She was able to get support from her church, as the pastor learned about the illness and responded to her in an understanding way.

Janet's is a fairly typical case, but sometimes the church leaders are not very understanding, and many of these patients eventually stop attending church, as they do not feel welcome. As the disease progresses, there may be changes that cause the individual to look and act in a manner that some may find uncomfortable.

Cognitive impairment is slowly progressive, usually over many years.

The disease does not affect naming, motor skills (including how to do things), or day-to-day memory.

It can affect working memory—multitasking, for example.

It affects executive function—decision-making capacity, judgment, organization, planning, goal setting, set shifting (changing from one set of circumstances to another), anticipation, and reasoning.

It affects "theory of mind" function—it's hard to take perspective, to surmise what others might be thinking, or to understand the feelings of others or how they might feel in a particular situation.

Treatment

Medication is the most important part, but there also is a need for psychosocial support—often housing and help with managing life. Many need to be in a supportive living environment, with family or in a group-living situation. Some are able to make it on their own. Only about 15 percent can maintain some level of employment. Some may be doing well into their twenties and then develop the symptoms, after having married and maybe with children. An understanding of the illness by those in the individual's social circle is vital.

The church needs to have an appropriate way to respond to members who are dealing with this illness but often do not understand how best to help. There may be episodes of bizarre behaviors, unusual responses to questions, impulsive speech at times, and maybe some symptoms of acute illness. It is important to recognize what is illness and what is from the individuals themselves. It is important to be able to love and accept them at whatever state they are in and not to overreact to unusual, benign behaviors or responses. Individuals often are confused over beliefs, especially when delusions might cause them to think that God has a special mission for them or that they have special powers, like healing; they may think they are God or Jesus.

It is important not to challenge the delusions. When the delusions and other symptoms interfere with their lives, help them to get the psychiatric help that they need.

Mortality associated with schizophrenia

High mortality rates in schizophrenia

- 1.6 times higher all-cause mortality risk
- 4.3 times higher risk from unnatural causes (e.g., suicide, accidental death)
- 1.4 times higher risk from natural causes (in particular from cardiovascular, infectious, respiratory, and endocrine disorders)

Overall life expectancy is 20% shorter than that of the general population.

Dixon L et al. J Nerv Ment Dis. 1990;490-502.

Harris EC et al. Br J Psychiatry. 1998;11-43.

Newman SC et al. Can J Psychiatry. 1991;36:239-245.

Trauma

What happens when major trauma disrupts the family? What is trauma? How do we define it? We know that a major incident, such as an earthquake or tornado, can devastate one's life, take away all one's goods, and have a major effect on the family.

The effect of trauma on an individual depends on several factors: the severity of the trauma, the context of the trauma, sense of threat to self or bodily harm, presence of hopelessness, the resilience of the victim, prior trauma, ability to respond or resist, psychosocial support afterward, and underlying mental or physical disorders. Trauma to one person might not be trauma to another, depending on the circumstances outlined above.

While we were working in Kenya during our first year, we lived in the bush, helping to develop primary health care in a village that had been devastated by drought and famine. Our housekeeper was a young lady who, unbeknownst to us, had been sold to a husband for a number of cows. One day, the brothers and the intended groom came to our house to forcibly take her back to her village. The young men had a number of weapons, notably an AK-47, which was subsequently pushed through each of our louvered windows, pointed at our young children. Ellen, my wife at the time, noticed this and fearlessly went out to confront them.

They pointed the AK-47 directly at her, with threats that they would kill her if she did not give up Grace, the young lady. Ellen grabbed the barrel of the gun, shoved the gun into the stomach of the warrior, and informed him that she was going to get her husband. When they saw that she was that tough of lady, they must have decided that her husband was something quite fearsome. They took off running and did not come back.

Though threatened with death, Ellen was in control and was able to take charge of the situation; she did not feel helpless or overwhelmed. She did not suffer any symptoms thereafter, but later in life, when we were living in Mexico City, we had a home invasion—a group of men forced their way into the house, grabbed Ellen by the arm, and pushed her into the house at gunpoint. This time, she told me the gun was a 9 mm Glock. She was forced to sit in the living room while the house was robbed of anything of value. The plan was then to shoot her and leave.

I was a few blocks away, shopping with a visitor, and our son was next door with his friends. The men placed a bag over Ellen's head and cocked the gun. She was sure at that point that she was going to heaven very soon. There was no escape; she knew a rescue was hopeless. She did, however, want to tell the man with the gun about Jesus before he shot her, and she tried to think of the words to say in Spanish.

Just as the man was ready to fire, our dog, a cocker lab named Money, bit him quite hard in the heel. When he turned around to shoot the dog, Ellen threw the bag that was over her head across the room. He grabbed the bag and put it over her head again, gun still cocked as he prepared to shoot her. The dog again bit him and avoided the pointed gun as he ran around the room. This distracted the man again.

At this point, the neighbors sensed something was going on, and they began to beat on the door to be let in. The men grabbed their loot and ran out the door, catching a bus that conveniently was going by.

Ellen was helpless, unable to respond or protect herself, and powerless. She had nightmares for months and could not tolerate seeing a Glock on TV programs for many years, as it would set off flashbacks. Her response in the two situations was quite different.

Trauma can happen and likely will happen to most of us. We live in a corrupt, evil world where evil people reside. Satan's minions are working to make life as difficult as possible for the servants of God.

Trauma needs to be understood in the context of the person. It may have been a minor event, but the person may be changed by it. We may not think of it as traumatic, but the victim needs a chance to be understood and supported through the situation. We do not minimize the trauma of others; we work with them to get them through it by being understanding and trying to see it from their point of view. We might think the trauma is small or insignificant but it is important to others. Not understanding someone's trauma can result in the breakup of a relationship or marriage.

With severe or major trauma, a disorder called *post-traumatic stress disorder* (PTSD) may occur. The family member might be a first responder (emergency medical technician in the US, along with police or firefighters) or a soldier who has seen active duty. The family may have suffered a natural disaster—earthquake, fire, volcanic eruption, hurricane, tornado, tropical storm, cyclone—or a severe motor vehicle accident, or they may have seen something horrific.

How do we respond to the individual or family who has undergone a severe trauma? They need to talk about it soon after the event. It may be difficult for an untrained individual to listen to the recounting of severe trauma so care needs to be taken. If you become overwhelmed with what is being disclosed, request a break or time-out. If you are out of your depth, refer to a trained counselor, if available, or one more able to deal with the trauma. As a professional, I have listened to firsthand accounts of war trauma, 9/11 trauma, and trauma that first responders have seen. It is hard for me. Sometimes, I have had secondary symptoms from hearing about trauma and have to talk about it with my staff. It is not unusual for one to be traumatized by listening to a victim's disclosure of trauma.

We can try several things to understand trauma so that we can respond well to those who have experienced something difficult. This is important for the spouse and parent, as well as the pastor or church leader:

Listen. Active listening means being quiet and attentive and only using words that might help individuals express themselves, such as repeating a short sequence to help clarify, nodding the head, letting them express what happened, and summarizing and repeating back what they said.

Provide support. If trauma has resulted in the individuals needing further help, find counseling with a professional for them. Encourage family members or friends to stay with them. Find other things they might need.

Allow time to heal. Whether an individual suffers a major trauma or something that we might think is inconsequential, he or she needs time to heal. There are some events that individuals just will not get over. In severe trauma, people change; they are not the same afterward. Trust becomes difficult, and the world seems crueler than ever. They become afraid to do certain things, such as driving, if trauma resulted from a motor vehicle accident, or returning to work, if it was a work-related trauma. When trauma is so severe as to cause symptoms or changes in individuals, they likely are suffering from PTSD (post-traumatic stress disorder); in this case, professional help is needed, if available.

Be understanding. Things have changed; the world is not as safe as it was, and reactions will be different. There now might be certain dates during the year that provoke memories or symptoms. Fears may be irrational to others but make sense to the victim. Adjust to the changes, and be supportive toward improvement over time. Time does not heal the trauma, but it does help make it a bit less of an intrusive or a constantly present memory. A spouse who has been traumatized may be cold and distant for some time as the healing proceeds. Be patient; it is likely not your fault that your spouse is this way. It is due to the extreme emotions of the trauma and the recovery process. Give him or her the time and space to recover.

The world is corrupt and cruel. Satan has a hold on the world and is called the prince of the power of the air.

> As for you, you were dead in your transgressions and sins, in which you used to live when you followed the ways of this world and of the ruler of the kingdom of the air, the spirit who is now at work in those who are disobedient. (Ephesians 2:1–2)

Satan is powerful and is the author of much of the chaos in the world. He empowers world leaders, cruel factions, and those who victimize others, with no regard for them as individuals. We will see trauma increasing as the world proceeds toward the coming of our Messiah. We need to expect that things will not go smoothly. Our relationship with Christ does not mean we will live lives of peace and without conflict. In fact, as we stay firm and close with God, we will experience difficulties as we tell others about Him and as we live our daily lives in this corrupt world.

To be able to face trauma, we need to be strong in our faith, stay close to God, and always have on our armor.

> The Armor of God
> Finally, be strong in the Lord and in his mighty power. Put on the full armor of God so that you can take your stand against the devil's schemes. For our struggle is not against flesh and blood, but against the rulers, against the authorities, against the powers of this dark world and against the spiritual forces of evil in the heavenly realms. Therefore put on the full armor of God, so that when the day of evil comes, you may be able to stand your ground, and after you have done everything, to stand. Stand firm then, with the belt of truth buckled around your waist, with the breastplate of righteousness in place, and with your feet fitted with the readiness that comes from the gospel of peace. In addition to all this, take up the shield of faith, with which you can extinguish all the flaming arrows of the evil one. Take the helmet of salvation and

the sword of the Spirit, which is the word of God. And pray in the Spirit on all occasions with all kinds of prayers and requests. With this in mind, be alert and always keep on praying for all the saints. (Ephesians 6:10–18)

The above is the spiritual approach, but with severe trauma, the individual also needs to find a good counselor, if one available, who can help the individual professionally. Trauma can affect us in the entire biopsychosociospiritual realm. Severe trauma changes the brain, so that it does not function in the same way. It affects the entire family system, even though only one suffered the trauma. It can take away the individual's confidence and cause fears that make it difficult to do certain things. Most important, it can cause individuals to question their faith, God, and their purpose and to affect their relationship with Christ.

Understanding the aspects of trauma can help us, as a family and as a church, to respond more appropriately to the one suffering so that healing can take place.

Praise be to the God and Father of our Lord Jesus Christ, the Father of compassion and the God of all comfort, who comforts us in all our troubles, so that we can comfort those in any trouble with the comfort we ourselves have received from God. For just as the sufferings of Christ flow over into our lives, so also through Christ our comfort overflows. If we are distressed, it is for your comfort and salvation; if we are comforted, it is for your comfort, which produces in you, patient endurance of the same sufferings we suffer. And our hope for you is firm, because we know that just as you share in our sufferings, so also you share in our comfort. (2 Corinthians 1:3–7)

Trauma Disorders

Trauma refers to individuals having experienced something that affected them significantly in a negative way. Not all trauma will lead to PTSD, but when trauma affects them in a way that it interferes with their lives, they may have developed PTSD.

Post-traumatic stress disorder can occur if:

- They undergo a significant trauma outside normal human experience.
- They witness death or harm to others.
- During the course of that traumatic event, they have a sense of profound helplessness and loss of control.
- There is risk of loss of life or serious bodily harm to themselves or others.

They then may experience symptoms related to the trauma, which can include nightmares, flashbacks, anxiety reactions, and/or irrational fears or responses.

This may sensitize them to future traumatic events, and they may react to situations in which they are reminded of that event (or those events, in the case of ongoing abuse or trauma).

Symptoms may include:

- Anxiety attacks—sudden onset of unexplained, unpleasant arousal, in which they sense fear or excess worry.
- Mood swings—sudden changes in the mood state, usually brought about by reminders of the trauma.
- Nightmares—may be unrelated but of similar theme to the traumatic event or reenactment of the event, with or without accurate details. They may awaken with a fast heartbeat, sweating, or a sense of severe anxiety and fear, or they may feel overwhelmed with emotions and may not easily return to sleep.
- Flashbacks—reenactment of the trauma via visual hallucinations, smells, auditory hallucinations, or tactile hallucinations, all related to the trauma. Sometimes the flashbacks will bring them back to the traumatic event, where they may reenact what is going on.
- Triggers—any type of sensory input, visual, auditory, tactile, olfactory (smell) that reminds them of the trauma and then results in automatic responses of unusual reactions, exaggerated startle response, anxiety, panic, and aggressive behaviors, even to point

of dissociating and going into the flashback, as though they are, at the moment, experiencing the traumatic event and reacting to it without realizing it.

An example is smelling a particular perfume that a perpetrator was wearing when the trauma occurred, setting off a reaction of fear and anger.

One of my patients, a Vietnam vet, came to me with the unusual symptom—suddenly, while walking down the road, he hurled himself into a ditch and tried to cover himself with dirt. We could not discern the reason for this. We then discovered he had PTSD from his service years in Vietnam War, where he was around live enemy fire. A particular high-pitched noise occurred with incoming missiles. We explored if there might be a noise like that in his environment. He was finally was able to connect it to a local bird that had the same tone and almost sounded like an incoming missile. When we connected the dots, he was very relieved and taught himself not to react to the noise.

Therapeutic Approaches

To properly understand and treat trauma, as with the other disorders, we need to approach it in a biopsychosociospiritual manner.

Biologic/Medication Approach

The goal of medication is to treat symptoms that interfere with the life of the individual. Many symptoms are alleviated through counseling, but the more difficult symptoms often need intervention of psychiatric medications. Often, if the symptoms are severe, therapeutic approaches are not possible until the distress is relieved.

Symptoms that can be helped with medication include:

- Depression
- Anxiety
- Flashbacks
- Mood swings

- Rage
- Sleep disorders—nightmares, sleepwalking, behaviors during dreams (REM behaviors), insomnia, night terrors
- Panic attacks
- Dissociation

Therapy Approach

Medications will help in the short term and often allow the therapy to proceed. The goal of therapy is to resolve the symptoms to the best degree possible to allow attachment and development to proceed.

- Cognitive Behavioral Techniques: This type of therapy is to help the patient deal with misperceptions and cognitive distortions, which will help to provide a way that they can properly perceive what is going on in their lives, to see themselves in a more realistic way, and to persistently tell themselves the truth.
- EMDR (Eye Movement Desensitization and Reprocessing): This technique has several decades of effective use. It is based on an assumption that individuals need to connect both sides of the brain while processing trauma by alternatively tapping one leg and then the other or moving eyes from side to side. The therapist can help the client to safely process the trauma, learn techniques of putting the trauma away when not discussing it in the session, and eventually come to the point that the memories and flashbacks no longer control the individual.
- Traditional Counseling: This involves slowly exploring the trauma in the past and connecting it to what is happening in current time. It involves supportive techniques that help strengthen a person's defense mechanisms (how he or she deals with stress and life). Expressive techniques are also used, including art and music, to assist with identifying feelings and working on ways to deal with what happened in a more balanced way. There is also psychoeducation, which involves helping individuals to understand their disorders and what happened to them.

- Other Approaches: There are many forms of therapy, and many are effective, but they mostly fall into the above categories. Counseling/therapy is effective and helpful.
- Precautions: It is very important that the counselor understands and has experience working with trauma. Sometimes when an individual is dealing with these very difficult memories, there is a phenomenon called *flooding*. This can be very dangerous, as the client is flooded with memories, feelings, flashbacks that result in severe anxiety, and sometimes self-destructive behaviors. If this occurs after sessions, the counselor needs to know, and the client needs to be monitored for suicidal or self-destructive behaviors and respond accordingly to keep him or her safe. If there is significant suicidal risk, hospital care may be necessary for a time.

Mental illness is common. Those suffering from these disorders need care, compassion, and proper treatment, as with any other serious health problem. As a church, we are the frontline for many who are seeking help. The church needs to be educated on how to best handle these situations. My hope is that the foregoing information will lead to many more individuals receiving the help that they desperately need.

18

The Heartbreak of Addictions

⟨~~⟩

One of the more prevalent destroyers of families is the problem of addiction. It is becoming more of a problem as time goes by. Anyone can be affected, and a number of newer addictions are attracting our attention. The church leaders and families need to be aware of these problems and design ways to help the individuals involved. It can affect children as well as adults and even the older population. According to some surveys, addictions are the sixth most prominent problem in the breakup of a marriage.

The addiction problem can be drugs or behaviors. Let's take a look at drugs first.

DRUGS

Quick Facts on Drug Addiction

- According to the National Survey on Drug Use and Health (NSDUH), 19.7 million American adults (aged 12 and older) battled a substance use disorder in 2017. (1)
- Almost 74% of adults suffering from a substance use disorder in 2017 struggled with an alcohol use disorder. (1)
- About 38% of adults in 2017 battled an illicit drug use disorder. (1)

- That same year, 1 out of every 8 adults struggled with both alcohol and drug use disorders simultaneously. (1)
- In 2017, 8.5 million American adults suffered from both a mental health disorder and a substance use disorder or co-occurring disorders. (1)
- Drug abuse and addiction cost American society more than $740 billion annually in lost workplace productivity, health care expenses, and crime-related costs. (2)
- Addiction affects every segment of our society and many families. Scientific studies have found that teenagers and people with mental health disorders are more at risk for drug use and addiction than other populations. (3)

(1) Substance Abuse and Mental Health Services Administration, Key Substance Use and Mental Health Indicators in the United States: Results from the 2017 National Survey on Drug Use and Health (2018).

(2) National Institute on Drug Abuse, Trends & Statistics (2017).

(3) National Institute on Drug Abuse, Drugs, Brains, and Behavior: The Science of Addiction (2018).

Drugs come in all kinds of formulations. There are so many different drugs that they could not be listed here, as new ones become available so quickly. The main categories are:

Opiates: These are narcotics. Many prescription forms are useful for pain when prescribed and used properly. The newer forms are particularly addictive and easily become deadly. For example:

Fentanyl
Morphine
Oxycodone
Hydrocodone

Nonmedical usage includes:

> Heroin
> Kratom
> Some variations of fentanyl (e.g., carfentanil)

Sedatives/hypnotics: Many are used for anxiety and sleep disorders. When prescribed and used properly, they can be very helpful in controlling symptoms and improving quality of life. When overused, the drugs produce a mental numbing and sedation, intoxication, and poor control of motor functions. They can become quite addictive when misused. Prescribed sedatives include:

> Valium (diazepam)
> Xanax (alprazolam), known on the street as Xanibars, which are 2-mg pills, a fairly high dosage
> Ativan (lorazepam)
> Klonopin (clonazepam)
> Dalmane (flurazepam)
> Restoril (temazepam)
> Ambien (Zolpidem)

Nonmedical usage includes:

> Alcohol
> Marijuana

Stimulants: Many of these can be used at low doses to help with attention deficit in adults and children, sleep disorders, eating disorders, and mood disorders. Abuse occurs generally at very high doses, which provides high energy, sleeplessness, agitation, anxiety, paranoia, delusions, and hallucinations.

Prescription stimulants include:

> Dextroamphetamine
> Methylphenidate

Nonmedical usage includes:

Methamphetamine
Cocaine
Some designer drugs

Hallucinogens: These are drugs that produce psychosis, abnormal perceptions and alterations in reality orientation. There are no prescribed usages, but there is work underway in looking at the use of some for assisting psychotherapy. For example:

LSD
PCP
Mushrooms
Psilocybin
Many new designer drugs

Behavioral Addictions

When we think of addiction, we immediately think of drugs, but there are behavioral addictions as well. They come in all forms:

Gambling
Sex
Pornography
Online gaming
Hoarding
Self-cutting (sometimes in the form of piercing and tattooing)

Pornography addiction has presented very serious problems, especially in the more developed countries. We have access to the internet in many places around the globe. Accessing pornography is so easy with only a click on the computer or phone. It may start out with curiosity or looking for a thrill. At home, the sex life might not so good, or one might be single. It can become an addiction for women as well as men, but it is more common in men.

After the first thrill, it is easy to crave another look and then another. Soon, individuals start using the pay sites, and money is lost. The thrill drives them deeper, looking to more graphic and more "exciting" types of sex. Observing this activity does not always lead to acting it out, but it has been implicated in many sexual crimes, including serial rape and murder. The depths of sin that can start with just a "look" can be unfathomable and horrid. This particular addiction has destroyed the testimony of ministry leaders, pastors, and teachers. It creeps into families, destroys and degrades the marital relationship, and leads to divorce, loss of the nuclear family, destruction of a career, and so much more.

The other behavioral addictions are serious but the potential consequences of a pornography addiction seem to be the worst of any of them. This seems to be one very potent weapon for Satan to use against us.

Sexual sin may start with pornography or just poor boundaries and impulse control. Our eyes often wander too far off track. Conversation might cross a boundary, then touching, and then progressing into intimacy. The addiction may be to multiple affairs, perverted sexual activity, homosexuality, or other outside-the-marriage activity.

Sex was designed by our Creator to be between the husband and wife—no one else. When we wander out of those important boundaries, we are at risk for serious consequences: loss of marriage, loss of trust, loss of relationship with Christ, depression, hopelessness, danger of suicide, or involvement in illegal activities.

Breaking the habit of behavioral addictions can be just as hard as with drugs. With the addictive behaviors, a thrill or a high often manifests in the brain, similar to what an addictive drug might do. After the first big thrill, there is the desire to chase the thrill, to look for it again. It takes more and more of the "drug" to feel satisfied. What occurs is the result from the law of diminishing returns; that is, seeking deeper and deeper involvement to find something close to the first thrill. It takes more and more to get to the level of that first thrill or high, much the same as with drug addiction.

Getting control of these addictions is similar to working with substance abuse but seems to carry a good deal more shame. With most of the above, the destruction of family, trust, and finances can be just as bad as the drugs—in some cases, worse. It is very important to recognize the danger signals early and try to get help as quickly as possible.

The concept of addiction is truly an extension of sin. In James 1:13–15, we read,

> Let no one say when he is tempted, "I am being tempted by God," for God cannot be tempted with evil, and he himself tempts no one. But each person is tempted when he is lured and enticed by his own desire. Then desire when it has conceived gives birth to sin, and sin when it is fully grown brings forth death.

There is first the enticement—an idea or mention by a friend of how good this activity or drug would be. There is a weakening of the will, a gradual wearing down of the sense of right or wrong, which most of us have instilled in us, whether we are believers or not. Then comes the moment when we yield to the desired activity. If we see that we are wrong and get out of it then, we suffer little damage. Most sin has an addictive component. Once we continue in that sin, it changes the brain—it become irresistible.

I strongly believe that with some—not all—of those who fall into addiction, there is demonic involvement that needs to be considered. I have seen this more often with the mind-altering drugs and sexual sin, particularly.

This is an avenue now where Satan and an individual's own willfulness combine to cause the sin to persist. The individual deeply feels the concept of truly being a slave to sin.

Breaking Free

How can we help addicts to break free?

The methods used in twelve-step programs are very helpful in the process of breaking free. The following are the main spiritual steps that need to be taken:

1. Acknowledge that you are a sinner, and you are addicted to _____.

2. Acknowledge that you are powerless over this addiction.

3. Acknowledge that you need the help of others and God to fully recover; you cannot do it on your own.
4. Accept Christ as your personal Savior (or if you already are a Christian, rededicate your life and return to Him).
5. Repent of the addiction and any other related sins.
6. Seek forgiveness from those hurt by your behaviors.
7. Find a trusted accountability partner who knows of your struggles and whom you can fully trust.
8. Come to understand that due to your powerlessness, you need to be involved in the process of recovery—active treatment and/or support to overcome the addiction—and that this needs to continue indefinitely.
9. If one is available, become involved in a recovery program, if your counselor, doctor, pastor, or spiritual leader feels you need that level of care.
10. Come to recognize that recovery is a lifelong process. You are always vulnerable to returning to the drugs or behaviors you left behind.
11. Adopt a recovery lifestyle—staying away from the triggers of the particular addiction, being accountable to someone, being humble, dealing with stress and feelings more appropriately, and seeking help when needed before the addiction gets out of control again.
12. Seek out others who are dealing with addictions to offer help to them via support groups or other venues.

Important Concepts

Usually, a person falls into addiction for a reason. Those who experiment as teenagers or young adults often are looking to fill something in their lives—loneliness, depression, boredom, wanting acceptance by peers, and so forth.

Some become addicted because of unresolved trauma. A common problem is growing up in an addicted family situation—someone in the family has an addiction, and this has the whole system in chaos. When the mother or father are not available to make proper attachment, there is a void. There is also a vulnerable change in the brain in which one finds little pleasure in relationships due to the attachment problem and seeks alternatives to fill that void.

Many are avoiding feelings. Living in a numbed-out state allows them to skirt the issues that might otherwise be difficult. Any time there is a feeling that's usually negative—high anxiety, grief, anger, disappointment, and so forth—there is a need to shut it down and not deal with it. For strong emotions, even elation from a positive experience, there is also a tendency to want to numb it to a more acceptable no-feeling state.

When recovery starts for some, it is a new situation, having to deal with life, feelings, and all. There often is a lack of language for feelings, poor coping strategies, and a tendency to being easily triggered back to the addiction so as to deal with life in the old manner. Overcoming these aspects often involves the support group type of connection—actually listening to others and responding to their feelings and recognizing your own. Group can also assist with developing coping strategies, but some individual counseling would be very helpful for this.

The church must be aware of the suffering of these individuals and how it affects the family and extended family when there is one who is addicted. Though many of the drugs used are illegal and individuals are considered criminals when they are in possession of those drugs, many are not really criminals but victims of their own addiction.

Compassion is needed but a firm hand is needed as well. If illegal behavior is involved, having the involvement of the court system can be very helpful—a sort of tough love to get people back on track. Having probation, incarceration, or other legal consequences sometimes serves to bring people back to the Lord—or to the Lord for the first time.

Sometimes, a sort of intervention is needed in which the addicted family member is confronted by loved ones and told of the destruction that is going on. They urge him or her to get into treatment. This is generally best set up by a professional who is knowledgeable in the process, as it can easily go wrong.

Pastors and church leaders must not shy away from visitation in the jail, prison, or psychiatric hospital when the opportunity arises. They need to be of assistance in bringing the wandering ones home to the Good Shepherd.

Church leaders need to be knowledgeable about the community resources for addictions, such as Celebrate Recovery, Pure Word, and inpatient recovery programs. (See the bibliography.)

Freedom in Christ

The Bible lets us know that the only true freedom is in Christ.

> It is for freedom that Christ has set us free. Stand firm, then, and do not let yourselves be burdened again by a yoke of slavery.
>
> —Galatians 5:1

19

Sin and Reconciliation: Wayward Children, Wayward Spouses

We know that the real cause of most of the problems in the family is sin. Sin separates us from each other. We all sin and must constantly look to Jesus for our own redirection to the right path. Some sin, however, is serious enough to put the family at risk of breakup. It may be a wayward spouse or a wayward child. Many times, professional intervention is needed. When this is available, it is so much better if a Christian counselor or psychiatrist is located. Sometimes, it falls completely to the church to provide the help.

The church has the job of reconciliation.

> All this is from God, who through Christ reconciled us to himself and gave us the ministry of reconciliation; that is, in Christ God was reconciling the world to himself, not counting their trespasses against them, and entrusting to us the message of reconciliation. (2 Corinthians 5:18–19)

If a family is dealing with strife and division, it is the job of the church to help them reconcile, be it a couple at war or a child who has found another path in life that will lead to destruction. Pastors and church leaders must learn biblical counseling to help in this area so that there can be healing and restoration.

Restoration

Restoration involves a willing and contrite heart and consists of confession; repentance; accountability; and restoration of the relationship with God, of the relationship with family and spouse, and to ministry, getting back to serving God.

Sin has a way of drawing us away from God and doing the right things. A family situation that often comes up is that one in the marriage has wandered off to seek someone else. Men as well as women are guilty of sexual sin. It starts with the eyes wandering where they should not, and then conversation starts and goes to areas it should not. Soon, there is a physical attraction and maybe all the way to the sexual act.

> When tempted, no one should say, "God is tempting me." For God cannot be tempted by evil, nor does he tempt anyone; but each person is tempted when they are dragged away by their own evil desire and enticed. Then, after desire has conceived, it gives birth to sin; and sin, when it is full-grown, gives birth to death. (James 1:13–15)

Many who have wandered off do not want to come back. They decide to leave the church and follow the person of their dreams, never listening to the Spirit and never coming under conviction for the sin. If there is no repentance, then not much can be done. Prayer for their conviction and return is the one thing we can do.

There are many cases, however, in which the offending spouse or child recognizes the error and wants to come back. Many times, I have seen the church turn her back on the person and not offer help. At that point, the offender is left hopeless. I also have seen the church work on restoring the sinner through a designed program to help him or her get back into full fellowship. If God can accept us back when we wander off, so must the church accept the repentant sinner who wants to return to the flock.

While working in Mexico City, I was serving as an elder in our small congregation. One of the worship team became involved with a woman other than his wife, and his wife discovered it. He came to the elders on his own to confess and to ask what to do. Together, we developed a program of restoration that worked well for him and others in the congregation. The basic format he followed was:

Confession: He recognized the sin and confessed it to God in the presence of the elders. He came to the elders first to let them know. He was removed from his duties at that point.

Repentance: He actively turned away from the sin, cut off the relationship, turned off the computer (if that was a problem), and gave up whatever was linked to the sin in question. He gave up any and all connections with the girlfriend.

Accountability: He accepted responsibility for the sin and developed accountability partners in the church to maintain the correct path. This meant talking with the accountability partner on a regular basis and whenever there were temptations or new problems. In his case, this was one of the elders.

Restoration of relationship with God: He entered into counseling with me on a weekly basis for the term of the restoration process. He was provided assignments from the pastor for devotional and scriptural readings and worked with him as well to draw closer to God.

Restoration of the marriage: Once he was making progress with his relationship with God and doing well with accountability, the marriage work began. They started marital counseling and had regular prayer and Bible-reading time.

Restoration to ministry: In his case, the process lasted about a year. At that time, the elders could see a changed man—humble, wife-loving, considerate, and ready to serve again with the worship team.

When considering any type of sin and the need for restoration, similar approaches can be used. We recall that Peter, after having denied Jesus three times, was restored by Jesus Himself.

> When they had finished eating, Jesus said to Simon Peter, "Simon son of John, do you love me more than these?"
>
> "Yes, Lord," he said, "you know that I love you."
>
> Jesus said, "Feed my lambs."
>
> Again, Jesus said, "Simon, son of John, do you love me?"
>
> He answered, "Yes, Lord, you know that I love you."

Jesus said, "Take care of my sheep."

The third time he said to him, "Simon, son of John, do you love me?"

Peter was hurt because Jesus asked him the third time, "Do you love me?" He said, "Lord, you know all things; you know that I love you."

Jesus said, "Feed my sheep. (John 21:15–18)

Jesus renewed his trust in the disciple by asking him a question three times. That became rather disturbing and allowed him to realize what had happened. Peter had to acknowledge his failure and reconnect to his Lord, assuring Him that truly he loved Him and would serve Him fully.

Brothers and sisters, if someone is caught in a sin, you who live by the Spirit should restore that person gently. But watch yourselves, or you also may be tempted. (Galatians 6:1)

Make sure that as we work to restore the fallen one that we stay close to God and that we are not guilty of the same things we are dealing with in the individual.

We all have that propensity to sin and fall away from God. We, as a church, must serve as a hospital for sick sinners to help them get back on board in their lives.

When children have decided to follow the world, we must confront this with a measure of *tough love.* That is, basically loving the sinners but hating the sin. Undergirded with prayer, we must confront the situation—first as a family and then with the help of church leaders—by meeting with the children and helping them to understand that they are heading to disaster with the choices they have made.

Today, the temptations for the children and adolescents are many. The world teaches a disdain for the Word of God and encourages many destructive behaviors. They are faced with gender confusion, homosexuality, drugs, resisting authority, atheism, and evolution, much of which is designed by the enemy to destroy the sure foundation of the Word. (See chapter 1.)

We must diligently work on preventive measures by openly teaching, in the youth groups and at home with devotions, what is right and proper. When there is confusion, we must help children to which direction would be best. This is done best with discussion, not with "laying down the law"—that is, we should not say, "This is right because I say it is right." Be open to discussing why it is right and what the consequences are to the decision and that God *always* looks out for our best interests.

Interventions can be arranged with professionals as well, especially when the child's behavior has led to the child becoming a danger to self or others. Any mention of suicide or behavior such as cutting or piercing needs professional intervention.

If there is criminal behavior, many countries have a juvenile court system that usually redirects the child and can be helpful. When the child spends some time "behind bars" or on probation, there is time to rethink and consider one's options. If this occurs, the youth leaders or pastor can be a strong influence in helping the child to adopt the best direction.

Both with children and adults, behaviors may be related to a mental illness. Children are vulnerable to mental health disorders, just as are adults. Some psychiatric disorders can lead to impulsive and out-of-control behaviors that look willful but may be the product of the mental disorder. The symptoms described in chapter 17 on mental illness can occur in children and adolescents as well. The most vulnerable or peak time for children to develop a severe mental illness is between ages twelve to fifteen and eighteen to twenty-one, not excluding other times they may develop.

Professional intervention is always necessary if signs or symptoms of a mental illness are present.

Restoring a wayward child can be similar to that of working with adults:

Confession: The child recognizes the sin and confesses to parents.

Repentance: The child actively turns away from the sin, leaving the relationships that may have encouraged the sin, and decides to follow the right path.

Accountability: The child accepts responsibility for sin and develops ways to be accountable to parents, pastor, and/or others. If it involves addiction, the child agrees to be in a recovery program, if available, and contracts to stay away from the areas of temptation—gaming, computer, phone, social media, friends, or other areas

Restoration of relationship with God: The child might need to establish a relationship with God, in which case the pastor or parents need to help with that, or his or her relationship might need to be restored. This is accomplished best with a personal devotional prayer time, as well as meeting with the pastor or a mentor to get back on track.

Soldiers in battle often speak of their commitment to leave no one behind. We are in a constant spiritual battle, and many become wounded, including our leaders, family members, and friends. Unfortunately, the church often leaves the wounded behind. We must strive to help those come back to the fold who are willing to be restored. We must not leave the wounded behind.

> But you, dear friends, build yourselves up in your most holy faith and pray in the Holy Spirit. Keep yourselves in God's love as you wait for the mercy of our Lord Jesus Christ to bring you to eternal life.
>
> Be merciful to those who doubt; snatch others from the fire and save them; to others show mercy, mixed with fear–hating even the clothing stained by corrupted flesh.
>
> —Jude 1:20–23

20

Finishing Strong: Keeping the Faith through the Challenges of Life

~*~

When hard times come, many, sadly, do not get through it successfully and draw away from God. As church leaders, we need to finish strong but also encourage our flock to finish strong. We do not want them to be stragglers. We all want to be victorious in our journeys and to finish strong.

The lion lies quietly behind the tall tuft of grass, carefully looking around. Ahead, he sees a herd of gazelle. They are grazing contentedly. They do not sense any danger. All is well. Just another day. The lion sees a tight group of adults, but outside of that group are some stragglers—some that appear weak and defenseless. He waits until the stragglers start to wander away, seemingly secure and feeling that no harm will come to them. The lion sees his chance. He carefully circles his intended prey, and just when they least expect it—the attack.

> Be alert and of sober mind. Your enemy the devil prowls
> around like a roaring lion looking for someone to devour.
> (1 Peter 5:8)

Who are the stragglers? Those who wander away from the herd. They may be those who have become weighed down with sin and temptation or those who have been afflicted by illness or mental illness. They may be those who feel they can do fine without the herd; they are proud and feel they are fine without the shepherd. The lion—Satan—and his minions are looking for stragglers whom he can devour, destroy, draw away from God.

In the herd, we are strong. The lion looks at those and figures there is no chance—we are supporting and caring for each other. There is no way for him to break into that group and get a meal. In the herd, we are family; we spur each other on to be strong.

Outside the herd, there is no support, no strength, no protection.

> Resist him, standing firm in the faith, because you know that the family of believers throughout the world is undergoing the same kind of sufferings.
>
> And the God of all grace, who called you to his eternal glory in Christ, after you have suffered a little while, will himself restore you and make you strong, firm and steadfast. To him be the power for ever and ever. Amen. (1 Peter 5:9–11)

We started this book with the basics of developing a foundation, structuring a family, raising the children, and then dealing with the hard stuff of life. The journey of life is difficult for anyone, as we all face struggles, challenges, and disappointments along the way—some far more than others. We need to keep in mind that we were created for a purpose.

> For we are God's handiwork, created in Christ Jesus to do good works, which God prepared in advance for us to do. (Ephesians 2:10)

When we finish our course, we will then hear those precious words that we longed for:

> "Well done, good and faithful servant.
> In order to make it safely through life, it is necessary to maintain the following:

Balance in Life

Balance is important in many areas of life. We all need to make sure our lives are built on the sure foundation of Jesus Christ and have him as our King, Savior, example, teacher, and brother. He is number one.

What are our priorities in life? Do we value anything above our relationship with Christ? Even the best of us have to keep correcting our courses. Our job becomes a priority, family issues try to override, money can become a focus, and even pleasure can draw us away from the real priorities of life. We have to continually correct our course:

> Therefore, since we are surrounded by such a great cloud of witnesses, let us throw off everything that hinders and the sin that so easily entangles. And let us run with perseverance the race marked out for us, *fixing our eyes on Jesus*, the pioneer and perfecter of faith. For the joy set before him he endured the cross, scorning its shame, and sat down at the right hand of the throne of God. Consider him who endured such opposition from sinners, so that you will not grow weary and lose heart. (Hebrews 12:1–3, emphasis added)

Our priorities must be:

1. God (our relationship with Him, His will, His direction)
2. Family
3. Ministry or job

We need to know our vulnerabilities and limitations, maintain good boundaries, and live close to Jesus.

It is very important that we strive to do the following:

*   Maintain personal and professional boundaries.
*   Understand our vulnerability and how Satan can make use of us if we do not stay close to Jesus.
*   Claim our strength through the Holy Spirit to complete our tasks.

Spiritual Habits

In order to run a race, compete in an athletic event, or take on an arduous hike, we have to be in shape. To take on the Christian life, it is the same. We are in a battle from the beginning until we are called home. Many mistakenly live their lives as stragglers, attending church on Sunday and living a worldly life all week, no different from anyone else. They think, *When life gets tough, then I will call on God for help.* The truth, however, is that if you are not in the habit of calling on God for daily help, you may not remember to call on Him when difficulties come. You will keep on trying to get through the problem on your own, but you will fail and then blame God for your trials.

Communication should be a spiritual habit:

- A healthy spiritual life revolves around communication—vertical with God and horizontal with our fellow travelers.
- We should regularly read the Bible, studying and applying what it teaches us. This is God communicating with us, guiding us, and keeping us on track.
- Through our prayer life, we communicate with God, telling Him our troubles, asking His help for our lives and our decisions, and for His mercy as we fall ill, or our loved ones develop serious health issues or other challenges.
- We worship together with our brothers and sisters as we are instructed in Hebrews 10:23:

  Let us hold unswervingly to the hope we profess, for he who promised is faithful. And let us consider how we may spur one another on toward love and good deeds, not giving up meeting together, as some are in the habit of doing, but encouraging one another —and all the more as you see the Day approaching.

  Rejoice always, pray continually, give thanks in all circumstances; for this is God's will for you in Christ Jesus. (1 Thessalonians 5:16–18)

A psalm. For giving grateful praise.
Shout for joy to the LORD, all the earth.
Worship the LORD with gladness;
come before him with joyful songs.
Know that the LORD is God.
It is he who made us, and we are his;
we are his people, the sheep of his pasture.
Enter his gates with thanksgiving
and his courts with praise;
give thanks to him and praise his name.
For the LORD is good and his love endures forever;
his faithfulness continues through all generations.
(Psalm 100)

Psalm 100 illustrates three principles in our relationship with God:

1. Humility: This is our standing before God. We are His children, and because of Jesus, we are forgiven. Our rightful place is as a servant, humbly bowing before our loving Father, listening to Him, considering Him as our God, taking ourselves off the throne and giving it to Him. "It is He who has made us, and we are His." One translation states, for the second part of the verse, "and not we ourselves." We sometimes can become so proud as to not humbly realize that He is our maker and redeemer.

2. Praise: This is uplifting God, placing Him back on the throne, regaling His many wonderful attributes, and acknowledging His power and glory. We do this often with worship songs and hymns, by our work, by doing our very best, by always recognizing Him in our daily walk, by feeding our minds with holy topics, and by keeping our eyes away from the world's temptations.

3. Thanksgiving: This is recognizing that He is our provider, and all good things come from Him. He is not only our maker but our provider. We bow in reverence and thanksgiving for our food, thanking Him daily for our strength and His mercies and grace toward us.

Since I accepted the Lord many years ago, I have always endeavored to pray before meals, especially when my family was with me. When eating alone, it was much easier to forget to do that, but when the family was with me, we always prayed before meals. This sometimes attracted attention when we prayed in restaurants. It was not negative attention, but others would come to join us, or people would stop to say how nice it was for us to pray, as though it was a strange and new thing. Apparently, many have forgotten this important ritual.

Recently, as we were about to pray in a restaurant, the waitress hurried over and asked us to pray for her. She was facing a very difficult situation in her life. Of course, we prayed for her. This was not the first time this happened—and hopefully it was not the last time. While living in Mexico a number of years ago, we had a favorite Japanese restaurant where we often ate. We always prayed before our delicious meal.

About a year after we started going there, the owner suffered a great loss. He was robbed and lost everything. He searched all over town for several days to find us. As a Buddhist, he did not have any faith in God, but he'd seen our faith, and when he finally found us, he asked us to pray for him because of his loss.

We were able to help him financially to restart, but his main consideration was to ask for prayer. His son soon started attending worship and studying with the pastor. He came to faith, but I never heard if his father had. Our expression of thanksgiving can have some powerful consequences!

To maintain our relationship with God, we must:

- Study the Word.
- Pray continually.
- Worship together.
- Be thankful, and always express our gratitude to our Provider.
- Serve one another in love.

Burnout

Sometimes the road gets very rough, and we may find ourselves in a state of exhaustion. We have spent too much energy on work, stressful situations, ministry, or other tasks and have not replenished the spent energy. When life is out of balance, we might be in a state of *burnout*.

Burnout is:
- Emotional exhaustion
- Physical exhaustion
- Energy debt
- Physical neglect
- Spiritual neglect
- Vulnerability to mental illness
- Vulnerability to temptation

Symptoms of burnout include:
- Fatigue
- Decreased concentration and attention
- Decreased creativity
- Irritability
- Anger or rage
- Low tolerance for frustration
- Lack of drive
- Desire to run away (even adults want to run away sometimes)

This can lead to serious stress in relationships. The vulnerability to temptation may result in one or both individuals in a couple seeking comfort and pleasure outside the bonds of marriage. One may find oneself addicted to drugs, pornography, gambling, or other things, ultimately causing a destructive downward spiral. It is important to be alert for the signs and symptoms of being out of balance so as to prevent the subsequent complications and consequences.

If an individual is caring for a spouse, child, parent, or close relative who is ill, especially with a chronic illness, caregiver stress can lead to burnout. The couple must be aware of the dangers, as must the shepherds in the church, who can help with rebalancing life.

Steps to Health

The Bible provides guidelines for how we can get life back into a balance and decrease the danger of falling away.

> Those who trust in the Lord are like Mount Zion, which cannot be shaken but endures forever. (Psalm 125:1)

Anxiety can become a problem if life is out of balance, but kind words can help relieve that.

> Anxiety weighs down the heart, but a kind word cheers it up. (Proverbs 12:25)

Giving to others, thinking about others, and refreshing others refreshes us.

> A generous man will prosper; whoever refreshes others will be refreshed. (Proverbs 11:25)

Those who have gone before us have left great examples for us to follow.

> Therefore, since we are surrounded by such a great cloud of witnesses, let us throw off everything that hinders and the sin that so easily entangles. And let us run with perseverance the race marked out for us, fixing our eyes on Jesus, the pioneer and perfecter of faith. For the joy set before him he endured the cross, scorning its shame, and sat down at the right hand of the throne of God. (Hebrews 12:1–2)

We need to keep our minds in shape. Like exercising the body, take each thought captive.

> We demolish arguments and every pretension that sets itself up against the knowledge of God, and we take captive every thought to make it obedient to Christ. And

we will be ready to punish every act of disobedience, once your obedience is complete. (2 Corinthians 10:5–6)

Turning away from sin and focusing on God helps us get on track.

Repent, then, and turn to God, so that your sins may be wiped out, that times of refreshing may come from the Lord. (Acts 3:19)

Even Jesus took time to pause and rest.

The apostles gathered around Jesus and reported to him all they had done and taught. Then, because so many people were coming and going that they did not even have a chance to eat, he said to them, "Come with me by yourselves to a quiet place and get some rest." (Mark 6:30–31)

Priorities

As mentioned above, our priorities must be reestablished:

1. Our relationship with God
2. Family
3. Ministry or job

Getting life back in balance involves putting energy into reordering our priorities. The first item on the following list is number one because the others will not happen unless we take control of our time.

1. Time management
2. Restoring regular devotional time
3. Restoring and maintaining confidence in God through worship
4. Restoring and maintaining important relationships
5. Managing anger and frustration
6. Restoring a positive attitude
7. Returning to a positive energy balance

Negative Energy

A number of things in normal life *consume* energy. We need to look carefully at our own lives to see what might be using up our energy. These might include:

- Conflicts
- Dealing with people, in general, or difficult people, in particular
- Heavy schedule; feeling rushed
- Lack of sleep
- Poor nutrition
- Tension, anxiety, worries
- Ministering to or caring for others
- Other (Consider what might be consuming your energy.)

Positive Energy

Energy debt needs to be paid. Our expenditure of negative energy needs to be paid for with positive input. What kinds of things in your life *provide* energy and give you a positive boost?

Seek things that are positive and that will restore expended energy. We all have different things that will restore energy and refocus our priorities— listening to music, watching a good movie, talking with friends, sharing a meal with family away from home, camping, picnicking, taking a walk, reading a good book, and so forth.

We each need to find what helps us to refocus and get back to fully functioning.

The following page shows a mnemonic that might be helpful. The page may be copied to use as a handout to church members who are struggling with keeping life in balance.

Larry E. Banta, M.D.

STRESS

Seek God: Find ways to connect in prayer and Bible study, associating with God's people in worship and praise.

Talk: Communicate with others, sharing your feelings, troubles, worries, and concerns. Or just talk over a cup of coffee or a meal. Dare to also share your dreams, ideas, and inspirations.

Relax: Find ways to reduce tension—read a book, engage in a hobby, listen to music.

Exercise and Eat Right: Treat your body right—fifteen minutes of exercise, three times per week, can make a big difference. Change your diet to more healthful choices with less saturated fat, lower carbs, more protein, and lots of fruits and vegetables.

Smile: Look for the humor in life—enjoy a funny story, watch an uplifting movie, or laugh together with someone special.

Sleep: Make sure you get the amount of sleep you personally need. We are all different, but the normal is between six and ten hours per night. Seek professional help if you are not getting restful sleep. Avoid caffeine late in the day, after 3:00 or 4:00 p.m. for most people. Develop good sleep hygiene.

From *Help for the Hurting Child*, Bookside Press (2022).

Consider using the following questions to explore how you are doing:

> What are your priorities?
>
> Is Jesus number one?
>
> How is your relationship with Christ?
>
> Is sin blocking your communication with God? Confess it to Him; He will forgive and put you back on track.
>
> What is consuming energy in your life?
>
> How can you restore that energy?

Don't be a straggler; the enemy is waiting.

For those who are struggling with challenging conditions and situations, the following paragraph can be used to encourage them to continue, to not give up, and to keep serving and loving, in spite of but sometimes because of an infirmity.

Holding together and keeping a balance are very important. Staying close to God keeps us going in the right direction, but finishing strong also has to do with maintaining an attitude of service to God, as much as we can, given our circumstance and general health. We must maintain a sense of being *well*, even if we are challenged with age or infirmity.

Are You Well?

In John 5:5, Jesus asks a pertinent question. A paralytic had been coming for years to the healing pool called Bethesda. Anyone who got into the pool first could be healed of their affliction. He had been paralyzed—that is, not well—for thirty-eight years.

Jesus asks him, "Do you want to be well?"

You might think, *Of course he wants to be well*. However, in my many years of work as a physician and psychiatrist, I have seen many situations where someone who was rather ill—generally, chronically ill—did not seem to want to be well. If I asked them that question, they would say that, of course, they wanted to be well. But did they really want to be well? They would often not follow instructions or not do the things that would help them get better or back on track.

What is *wellness*? That becomes the real question.

This is the true story of an eleven-year-old girl who was brought into a hospital in Thailand for rather severe bone pain. It was discovered she had metastatic bone cancer. She underwent amputation of the leg with the primary tumor, but this did not stop the progression, and she eventually passed away. During her several-week stay in the hospital, she managed to lead one doctor and several nurses to faith in Christ. She maintained a joyful, grateful attitude, undoubtedly from the Holy Spirit that indwelled her. She spoke each day of her faith and sang songs to the nurses and the doctor. Eventually, they asked about her faith, so she told them. She was a whole person, fully serving her Lord, all the way to the end of life.

Being well may not mean we are perfectly healthy and strong. We may have a chronic condition that won't improve, or we may just be older and not as strong as we were when we were young; we have some limitations. But are we well? Maybe that question could be better stated as, are we *living* well?

I taught a seniors class for many years at our local church. I asked one of my eighty-eight-year-old members if he could help out on a particular project. He pulled out his calendar, looked it over, and remarked that maybe he could fit it in. He had been retired for many years, but his week was filled with helping out where he could. I admired that. He had the attitude, "If I am still alive, I can still be of use to God."

In an earlier chapter, I wrote of my wife, Ellen, who suffered from MS and dementia and eventually had to live apart from me in a nursing facility for several years. One day, as I came into her room at the facility, I saw her with one of the male aides. They were holding hands and were in a deep, reverent prayer. I thought, *How kind of him to come and pray for her.*

Actually, as I later learned, he and many others would come into Ellen's room when they had a moment, and *she* would pray for *them*! Her tablemates at dinner were all believers but one. They would talk of God and heaven at dinner. I found out that her next-door neighbor, one of her tablemates, was very ill and was at the point of dying. I knew Ellen needed to see her. I asked the nurse to make sure that Ellen could get in to be with her neighbor. She was wheeled into the room to be with her neighbor in her last moments. Ellen spent a lot of time telling her friend about heaven and that with her trust in Jesus, she would be there with Him soon. She passed away not long afterward. Ellen, at this point, was a woman who could not get out of bed, could no longer walk, and her brain was not working particularly well, but she allowed God to use her, even in her own last days.

How about you? Are you living well? Do you have an attitude of humbleness before God to allow Him to use you in whatever circumstance you might be in? It is not easy, but if you have your mind on heaven and know that this is a temporary home and that our suffering will soon be over, it becomes more possible for us to be used here on earth while we can.

Finding Peace

One other issue in finishing strong is having peace in our lives. If we do not experience the peace that God offers, we may look for it in the wrong places. We all want peace, but in this world, there is no real peace without having a relationship with God.

Jesus gives us peace, and knowing this can settle our hearts.

> Peace I leave with you; my peace I give you. I do not give to you as the world gives. Do not let your hearts be troubled and do not be afraid. (John 14:27)

There is trouble here in this world, but we have peace as we trust in Him.

> I have told you these things, so that in me you may have peace. In this world you will have trouble. But take heart! I have overcome the world." (John 16:33)

We need to put our minds on God, not on our fleshly desires.

> Those who live according to the flesh have their minds set on what the flesh desires; but those who live in accordance with the Spirit have their minds set on what the Spirit desires. The mind governed by the flesh is death, but the mind governed by the Spirit is life and peace. (Romans 8:5–7)

In finding peace, we first commit our lives to Christ, allowing His Spirit to dwell within us. Then, we choose to live for Him. In our journey through life, we will encounter all kinds of difficulties and strife. There is so much that will draw us away from a walk with Christ. As we divert from Him, we start trusting in ourselves, in our power, and we make decisions without consulting Him. Then the turmoil comes.

I have heard many people say that they don't pray so much, but they will call on God if a big problem hits. I have worked in the emergency room, where big problems hit and individuals' lives are on the edge. Those who have practiced prayer all of their lives have little difficulty lifting their problems to God. Those who have not practiced prayer end up in fear and dread of what will happen, and they are clearly not at peace.

> Cast all your anxiety on him because he cares for you. (1 Peter 5:7)

If we practice our faith daily, it becomes an ordinary part of life. I have had the opportunity to be around some very mature Christians and have been able to observe their lives; I've tried to pattern my own life to be like theirs. As soon as they hear of a problem with someone in their family or friends or among themselves, they go before the throne, seeking God to have guidance, help, and peace through the storm. We must keep casting our anxieties on Him, and He will give us peace because He cares for us!

Peace, then, comes with practicing holiness and focusing our lives on Him, and when we do veer away from Him, we return quickly to the path.

Unless Jesus comes first, we will face the end of our days here on earth. May we all share in the words of Paul:

> I have fought the good fight, I have finished the race, I have kept the faith. Now there is in store for me the crown of righteousness, which the Lord, the righteous Judge, will award to me on that day —and not only to me, but also to all who have longed for his appearing.
> —2 Timothy 4:7–8

21

A Word about Persecution

In various parts of the world, our brothers and sisters are undergoing persecution. If it has not hit your area, it likely will. Satan is busy, trying to discourage and divert as many of us as he can.

> Blessed are those who are persecuted because of righteousness, for theirs is the kingdom of heaven. (Matthew 5:10)

The previous lessons on laying a good foundation and keeping life in balance are certainly important. With that foundation in place, we can call on God to get us through, to give us the words that will help and the strength to endure. Expecting something and mentally preparing for it can be very helpful. Know in your heart that you will not betray the Savior.

When my children were young, we traveled into areas that were experiencing persecution. We never experienced any hardships but met many who had. We told our children early on, "If anyone threatens your life by saying you must give up your relationship with Christ or die, you must stand firm. You know where you are going from here. Keep that in mind. If anyone tells you they will kill or torture your parents or your sister or your brother, your answer must be the same: we know where we are going. Do not deny your Savior!"

I can only imagine what it must be like to undergo the persecution that many of our brothers and sisters have endured. Those who survived and came through had managed only with the strength from the Holy Spirit within them. It was not humanly possible, in many of the circumstances, to endure and maintain.

As the expected persecution comes, be sure to stand firm, and hold on to Jesus. He will give you the words to say and the courage to stand, as so many before you have.

Resources from the Voice of the Martyrs can be very helpful, if and when this becomes a reality in your life and in the lives of those in your congregation. The Voice of the Martyrs is an organization that works with the persecuted church worldwide with resources to help those who have been driven from their homes, are in prison, or have lost loved ones or other situations related to persecution. Their website is found at www.vom.org.

> Be on your guard; stand firm in the faith; be courageous; be strong. (1 Corinthians 16:13)

> Therefore, my dear brothers and sisters, stand firm. Let nothing move you. Always give yourselves fully to the work of the Lord, because you know that your labor in the Lord is not in vain. (1 Corinthians 15:58)

Bibliography

Included with the bibliography is a suggested list of resources, provided by trusted counselors and therapists. Always be like the Bereans and check out any resource to see if it follows God's Word and is not contrary to our foundational beliefs.

> Now the Berean Jews were of more noble character than those in Thessalonica, for they received the message with great eagerness and examined the Scriptures every day to see if what Paul said was true. (Acts 17:11)

Balswick, J & J. *The Family*. Grand Rapids: Baker Books, 1999.

Banta, Larry E., MD. *Effective Orphan Care Ministry, Rock Solid Kids to Rock Solid Adults.* Create Space Independent Publishing, 2015.

Banta, Larry E., MD. *Help for the Hurting Child: Christian Approaches to Therapeutic Parenting.* San Diego, CA: Bookside Press, 2022.

Banta, Larry E., MD. "Mental Illness in Two Rural Kenyan Outposts." In *Mental Health in Africa and the Americas Today*, edited by Samuel Okpaku. Nashville, TN: Chrisolith Books, 1991. The chapter tells the story of dealing with unresolved grief in tribal Kenya.

Barna, George. *Transforming Children into Spiritual Champions*. Delight, AR: Gospel Light Publications, 2003.

Bee, Helen, and B. Bjorklund. *The Journey of Adulthood.* Upper Saddle River, NJ: Prentice Hall, 2004.

Benokraitis, N. *Marriages and Families—Changes, Choices, and Constraints.* Upper Saddle River, NJ: Prentice Hall, 2002.

Chapman, Gary. *The 5 Love Languages.* Northfield, MA: Northfield Publishing, 2017.

Chapman, Gary, and Ross Campbell. *The 5 Love Languages of Children.* Chicago: Moody Publishers, 1997.

Copeland, A., and K. White. *Studying Families.* Newbury Park, CA: Sage Publications, 1991.

Corey, Gerald, et.al. *Issues and Ethics in the Helping Professions.* Independence, KY: Cengage Learning, 2018.

Crabb, Larry. *Marriage Builder: Creating True Oneness to Transform Your Marriage.* Grand Rapids, MI: Zondervan Press, 2013.

Dobson, James. *What Wives Wish Their Husbands Knew about Women.* Carol Stream, IL: Tyndale Press, 1975.

Diagnostic and Statistical Manual 5th Edition. Washington, DC: American Psychiatric Press, 2013.

Eisenberg, Eric. *Organizational Communication.* Boston, MA: Bedford/St. Martin, 2017.

Gray, John. *Men Are from Mars, Women Are from Venus.* New York: Harper Collins, 1992.

Hamner, T., and P. Turner. *Parenting in Contemporary Society.* Needham Heights, MA: Allyn & Bacon, 2001.

Hunter, James. *The Servant, A Simple Story about the True Essence of Leadership.* Currency, 2008.

Mindel, C., and R. Habenstein. *Ethnic Families in America.* Upper Saddle River, NJ: Prentice Hall, 1998.

Papalia, D., and S. Olds. *Human Development.* Boston, MA: McGraw-Hill, 1998.

Sell, C. M. *Transitions through Adult Life*. Grand Rapids, MI: Zondervan, 1991.

Sherman, D., and W. Hendricks. *Your Work Matters to God*. Colorado Springs, CO: Navpress, 1987.

Simpson, Amy. *Troubled Minds, Mental Illness and the Church's Mission*. Westmont, IL: InterVarsity Press, 2013.

Smither, E. *The Use of the Bible with Children*. New York, New York: Abingdon-Cokesbury Press, 1937.

Stewart, J. *Bridges Not Walls*. Boston, MA: McGraw-Hill, 2002.

Walker, Lenore E. *The Battered Woman*. New York: Harper and Row, 1979.

Whitfield, C. L. *Healing the Child Within*. Deerfield Beach, FL: Heath Comm., 1989.

Wright, H. Norman. *101 Questions to Ask before Getting Engaged*. Eugene, OR: Harvest House Publishers, 2004.

Wright, H. Norman. *Before You Say I Do*. Eugene, OR: Harvest House Publishers, 2009.

Websites

Alzheimer's Association offers help and information with Alzheimer's and other dementia: https://www.alz.org, and www.alzheimers.org.uk.

Association for Frontotemporal Degeneration offers help and information about this challenging disorder: www.theaftd.org.

American Parkinson's Disease Association: www.apdaparkinson.org.

Brain Injury Association of America: https://www.biausa.org.

Child Evangelism, leading your child to Christ: https://www.teachkids.eu/pdfs/ucan_lead.pdf.

Finances and Money Management: crown.org, and ramsaysolutions.com.

Food budgeting: https://spendsmart.extension.iastate.edu/plan/what-you-spend.

Frontiers Inc.: https://www.frontiersin.org. Brain imaging of depression and other mental illnesses.

Health Line: www.healthline.com. Diet and nutrition information.

Huntington Disease Society of America: http://hdsa.org.

Medical information: www.webmd.com.

Moms in Prayer International provides resources and help for parents who have children in the public schools and other issues: https://momsinprayer.org.

National Institute of Mental Health provides information for families and patients regarding all types of mental illnesses: https://www.nimh.nih.gov.

National Organization for Rare Diseases offers help in understanding and dealing with uncommon diseases: http://rarediseases.org.

National Multiple Sclerosis Society provides information and help for those suffering from multiple sclerosis: www.nationalmssociety.org.

Roman Road to Salvation: https://teenmissions.org/roman-road-to-salvation.

Sexuality Education: www.intoxicatedonlife.com.

Stroke Survivors Can provides information and encouragement from stroke survivors: https://strokesurvivorscan.org.

Stroke information, general: www.stroke.uk.

Taylor-Johnson Temperament Analysis (T-JTA): https://www.tjta.com.

The Voice of the Martyrs provides resources for churches and individuals under persecution: www.vom.org.

Domestic Violence Resources

Specific resources recommended by CBE International (https://cbeinternational.org).

1. *The Courage Coach* by Ashley Easter
2. *Healing Voices: Women of Faith Who Survived Abuse Speak Out* by J. Harris
3. *We Were the Least of These: Reading the Bible with Survivors of Sexual Abuse* by Elaine Heath
4. *Black and White Bible, Black and Blue Wife* by Ruth Tucker
5. *No Place for Abuse* by Catherine Clark Kroeger, Nancy Nason-Clark
6. *Ending Violence in Teen Dating Relationships* by Al Miles
7. *When Love Hurts: A Woman's Guide to Understanding Abuse in Relationships* by Karen McAndless-Davis and Jill Cory (Disclaimer: This book is not an explicitly Christian resource, but it has been vetted by CBE bookstore staff.)
8. *Domestic Violence: What Every Pastor Needs to Know* by Al Miles
9. *Breaking the Silence: The Church Responds to Domestic Violence* by Anne Weatherholt
10. *Strengthening Families and Ending Abuse* edited by Nancy Nason-Clark, Barbara Fisher-Townsend, Victoria Fahlberg

Addiction Resources

Focus on the Family (focusonthefamily.com) has a list of resources in many areas for Christian approaches to addiction.

The Gospel Coalition (thegospelcoalition.org) provides information and assistance with addictions, including pornography.

Celebrate Recovery (celebraterecovery.com) provides support groups in many churches in the United States.

Christian Recovery International (christianrecovery.com) has information regarding addiction and programs in many countries and various languages.

SAMHSA (https://www.samhsa.gov/find-help/national-helpline) helpline for those in US suffering from addiction and needing help.

SAMHSA (https://www.samhsa.gov) for general information regarding addiction.

About the Author

Dr. Larry Banta was born and raised in Ohio on a farm near Cincinnati. Upon graduation from high school in Lebanon, Ohio, he left for college in Lincoln, Nebraska, where he obtained a BS in microbiology. From there, he attended University of Nebraska Medical College, where he was awarded his MD degree. It was during his junior year in college that he was invited to church by his mother, a very new Christian, and heard the gospel for the first time. It was then his journey began, as he accepted Christ and was baptized.

He was married to his first wife, Ellen, in Nebraska during medical school. She was a missionary kid, having been born and raised in India. During medical school, he spent the last three months in India learning tropical medicine and helping to design a hospital there.

Following an internship in internal medicine and a two-year stint in the US Public Health Service on the Yankton Sioux Reservation, doing general medicine, the family moved to Kenya. Larry developed a clinic and managed several epidemics, including a severe polio epidemic in West Pokot for about a year. The next year was spent working in the mountains, developing a clinic, seeing patients, and preaching the gospel. A church was planted that has developed into many other congregations and an orphanage. Due to health concerns, they left Kenya after less than two years.

Returning from Kenya, Larry decided that he would train in psychiatry. He completed general psychiatry and a fellowship in child and adolescent psychiatry. The training included family therapy and working with many difficult family situations.

Over the years Dr. Banta has worked with displaced children, orphan care, and severe and chronically mentally ill adults and children, providing a varied, challenging, and rewarding ministry and career. He has provided family seminars in Kenya, Mexico, and the US.

In late 2017, Ellen passed away after a long battle with the multiple sclerosis. In 2019, Larry remarried to Evelyn, a licensed professional counselor. They work together on various projects related to mental health.

It is their prayer that this book will be widely distributed and serve to encourage pastors and those working with families in the local church so that the church remains strong and the families can pass along an active, productive faith to their children.

Acknowledgments

I wish to acknowledge the help and encouragement of so many who have made this book possible:

- John Van Kirk, for review of the manuscript and help with the references

- Dr. Paul Brand, who first planted the idea that working with making families stronger is of such importance for the church and society, and there was need for more help for families around the globe

- Paul Fine, MD, my family therapy supervisor so many years ago during my training, who taught me so much about families and children

- And my wife, Evelyn, who has been my support through the process of getting this finished